To Kaye, Hope you enjoy

WHAT IS QIGONG?

A step-by-step guide to growing a successful daily practice of Qigong

By Christopher David Handbury

Cover design and Illustration by Christopher David Handbury

Author's Disclaimer

This publication has been designed to provide information in regard to the subject matter covered. The author will not in any way be held responsible for any injury caused by the incorrect use or practise of the methods within this book. The techniques and methods detailed in this book are to be used at the reader's own risk.

The practice of Qigong is very safe when performed according to the advice given in this book. Cautions and advice have been provided where needed. The author recommends the guidance of a trained Qigong practitioner to provide the best possible experience of the information provided.

Readers are advised to seek professional advice or treatment for any medical conditions prior to undertaking a new form of health exercise or therapy.

The author does not recommend the practise of the Qigong in this book for those who are suffering with terminal illness, severe psychiatric conditions (e.g., severe depression, active suicidal ideation, schizophrenia) current severe medical conditions for which exercise is contraindicated, chronic addiction to alcohol and drug abuse, or for women who are pregnant.

Acknowledgements.

The information in this book has been gathered and compiled from my own experience of treating patients with Acupuncture, Qigong and Tui Na massage, teaching students and undertaking personal tuition from my respected teachers without whom this publication would not be possible.

I would like to convey my utmost gratitude to those who have made my journey more enjoyable and educational. Firstly, I would like to thank all the students who I have had the pleasure to meet and train with over the years. You have all helped me grow as a teacher and practitioner. Your dedication and support are an inspiration.

Secondly to the teachers who have given their time and knowledge to me over the years. I will continue to do my best to honour and share these great methods throughout my life.

Finally, I would like to thank my wife, Nicola, and my children, Tayla, Sophia and Isaac for your tolerance and acceptance of my passion for Qigong and teaching.

Contents

Foreword

Qigong means Energy Work and is part of a rich history of Chinese exercise. It offers a radically different approach in method and understanding. Over the last thirty years of experience in this field I have been constantly amazed at both the simplicity of the arts and the profound results they can create. Some are expected, and some are quite the surprise. Qi Gong is not for everybody, and not for every occasion. However, in nearly all cases it improves the situation, physically, emotionally and/or spiritually.

Beginning a journey into this art requires a certain commitment. There is no point in trying a single class or just reading a book; you must delve in and do the work. There is no such thing as a 'free lunch'. Traditional training methods suggest 100 consecutive days to get even an inkling of the effects of an exercise. Now that may seem like a long time, but it is only three months. It's a bit like rowing upstream, every time you stop, you go back a bit. It is easy at the beginning, everything is fresh and exciting. By the middle it can start to become more challenging. You will be tired, it can become routine, or even boring at times. This stage is crucial, you must keep going.

This is where *'What is Qi Gong?'* becomes invaluable. Christopher Handbury's clear enthusiasm shines through, as does his understanding and different theoretical approaches. I suggest once you start on the practical application of the book, go back and read it again, and then again. You may find the meaning of words changes along with the exercises.

Sifu Tony Dove

(Sifu Dove has 30 years' experience in Chinese Internal Arts under Grand Master Lam Kam_Chuen. He currently teaches Qigong and Tai Chi alongside his Traditional Chinese Medicine practice near Bristol, England)

Introduction

Firstly, let me start by saying thank you for opening this book. Whether you bought it, borrowed it, or found it, you have already taken a first step towards learning a very special and sometimes magical method of self-healing.

Within these pages I will teach you how to practise the healing art of Qigong and confirm how simple it can be to improve your health and happiness on a daily basis.

In my crusade to spread the teaching of Qigong and keep this great art alive, I have compiled this book as a reference manual for students and those seeking to begin a simple daily practice of Qigong.

The book is also a vehicle for me to share my knowledge and experience of my own journey and how Qigong has helped me to relieve the symptoms of physical and emotional pain that many of us will experience throughout our lives.

Over the past 15 years, Qigong has become embedded in my journey through life. It has helped me through illness and injuries, provided me with clear thinking to make life decisions and instilled a peace to my mind when the world around me has been noisy and overwhelming.

I think we can all agree that life can be tough sometimes and feeling tired, suffering with aches and pains or managing excessive amounts of stress and trauma can make it a very dull experience indeed.

Put simply, Qigong will help put the spring back into life when days feel heavy and hard to navigate. With a daily practice you can regain a sense of youthfulness that will help you enjoy life's moments with more zest and vitality, and the best thing is, it's simple and easy to get started.

If you are new to Qigong I hope you will find the information in these pages educational and inspiring. If you are already familiar with it but do not have a daily practice yet, then these pages will serve to guide you into a regular pattern of self-care and health development.

For those of you who have some knowledge of Qigong, please enjoy the methods and techniques I am about to share with you and feel free to incorporate this information into your existing practice.

‘Within all of us is a great power,
A natural desire to feel well and
enjoy life to its full potential’

Chapter One

The Perfect Triangle

Reconnecting Your Body and Mind

There are three main aspects to the Qigong within these pages that address our general needs for a balanced and healthy life.

1. Physical Development

2. Emotional Healing

3. Spiritual Nourishment

When these three aspects or 'qualities' are brought into balance, we have harmony and good health within our lives. Our health resistance becomes more durable and we are able to recover faster with less damage to the body and mind.

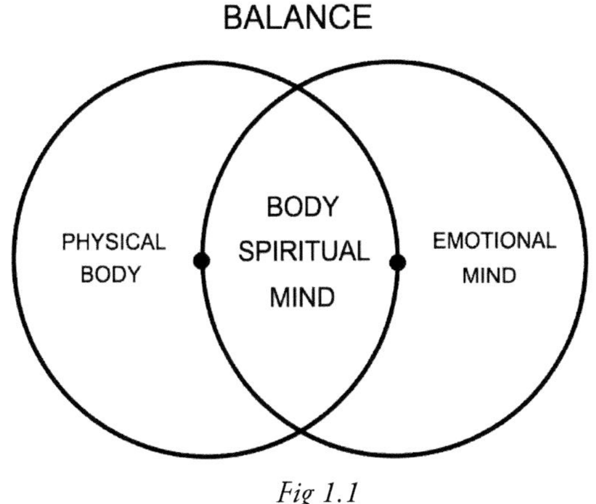

Fig 1.1

There are many health systems available that predominantly target the physical body, like sports and gym training. Similarly, there are practices that concentrate more on the emotional mind like vocal therapies, counselling and some meditation practices.

In order to improve the health of the entire body system in a holistic manner, it pays to address all three qualities to achieve the desired result. *(Fig 1.1)*

The most common complaints regarding health are mostly related to the physical body. Our aches, pains and injuries can be daily occurrences which hinder our enjoyment of life, so that is where we will begin our journey.

The Physical Body

The physical qualities of practice are related to the physical movements or active components of Qigong. They help to maintain the health of the muscles, bones and tissues much like many other forms of exercise.

The big difference with Qigong, as a physical exercise system, is not only are we maintaining physical health, we are also simultaneously learning to release physical tension in the body, which often causes the emotional stress and pain we feel on a daily basis.

Physical pain comes in many forms. From the acute trauma of knocks and bruises to the pain caused by lack of movement or stagnation of energy.

Inflammation of the joints and connective tissues has led to many modern illnesses and diseases that doctors cannot treat or do not have the time or resources to invest in to find a solution. There are also many painful conditions that can be caused by the emotions and our reactions to stress.

It is very rare that pain appears instantaneously. It may have started as a slight ache, feeling of tension or an uncomfortable movement. It may only manifest itself at certain periods during activities or even during certain seasons or weather conditions. These feelings of pain are usually the first signs that something is wrong.

It is very important to understand that addressing pain in the first instance is a responsibility that we must all take seriously, especially if we want to lead a healthy and pain-free life.

Taking action in the first stages can have an immense healing effect on whatever condition has started to manifest itself.

The Emotional Mind

Through our physical practice, we learn to release tensions and restrictions in the body. The result or effect of this is the mind begins to relax, become calm and provide space for the emotions to either be resolved or released.

This can be an immediate help with job stresses, family issues or even reducing the daily reminders of long-term trauma. Gradually the mind will become calm as the body relaxes and together, these two qualities can reconnect and help you to feel whole again.

The range of emotions we feel can be a rollercoaster of changes. Strong or distressing emotions are sometimes too much for the physical body to cope with and emotions that are not addressed early enough will eventually drain the physical body. *(Fig 1.2)*

This often results in our immune system becoming compromised and our muscles becoming weak because all of our energy and resources are being absorbed or utilised by the body and mind to prevent us from breaking down physically or emotionally.

Our amazing bodies are constantly adjusting, balancing and restoring our bodily functions so we can return to a more harmonious state of being. If the emotions are not nurtured and resolved in the initial stages of imbalance then we can enter into a chronic stage of suffering.

Over longer periods of time the emotions can also start to scatter and become unpredictable like the wind: rising, sinking and changing course or character.

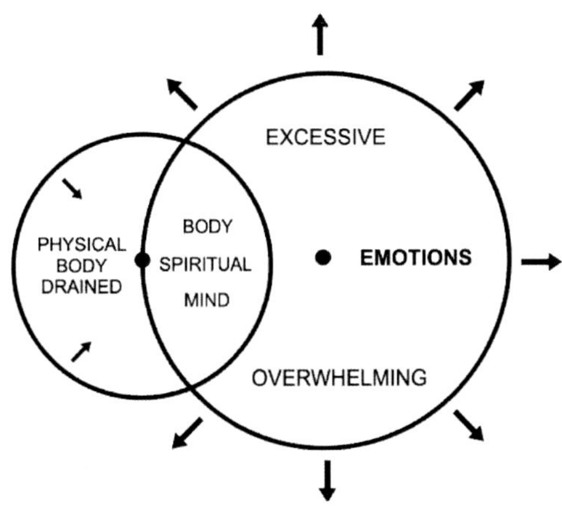

Fig 1.2

At this point it can be hard to see the true root of any illness so many of you will become confused and lose sight of your health goals.

It's not just those who suffer with long-term illnesses that are affected either. Many of us have become seasoned players at creating our own ill health, especially through physical damage. When the physical body has become weakened and deficient through overuse, there is only one clear option: stop; rest; and recover.

This deficiency can be caused by physical exertion, such as overtraining at the gym, working long hours, not taking enough rest or experiencing physical stress over a continuous period of time.

There will always be times when we will ignore these signs or deny our health needs attention. Life is never as rosy as we would like, so we adapt to the changes.

Temporary moments of denial are okay, but many people have become experts at ignoring their health. The 'mind over matter' attitude can be a great tool when used properly, but constant failing to listen to the messages sadly results in illness and more pain. Eventually a separation of the mind and body occurs, and we are lost.

During this process of separation, the physical body is weakened so much it often becomes the job of the emotions to step in and take charge to let you know something needs to change. This is often where fatigue, headaches, depression and pain conditions manifest themselves.

The body and mind are doing everything they can to shut you down to rest and heal. Finding the right solution at this time is paramount as these are the times when we lose our centre. This is when Qigong is a much-needed rescue remedy.

The Spiritual Self

The third quality is spiritual, which holds many different meanings for each individual through the different phases of their lives.

For me personally, spirituality is not a religious aspect of Qigong, although there are Qigong systems practised for religious reasons. Nor do I see spirituality as an esoteric idea of external beings or an entity separate from myself.

Over the years I have come to feel being spiritual is more about having a personal and honest relationship with yourself and how you care and nurture your physical, emotional and spiritual qualities. Having an awareness of your true feelings and being honest with yourself is my kind of spirituality.

I also feel too much time is wasted trying to find the 'real' you. This seems like a very 'new age' thing to do especially when you are in conflict with your health and emotions. The best thing is, once you get the first two aspects of Qigong right then the third aspect tends to grow naturally within you. There is no real need to find a deserted island or climb a mountain to find the 'true' you, because YOU are already there!

You just need to get rid of life's rubbish, reduce the emotional or physical noise, and allow the spiritual aspect to grow. Simple.

Once you have relative balance, *(Fig 1.3)* the relationships within us change and all three aspects are equally nourished. When this happens, we begin to grow with good, balanced health and the enjoyment of everyday life becomes our focus for living.

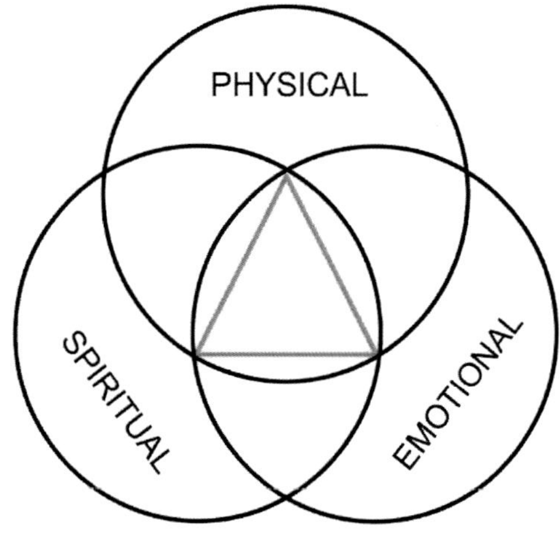

Fig 1.3

Okay, now we have a basic idea of how our health can be affected and what we are working with, let's look at some of the basic needs of those seeking better health and well-being, and why Qigong could provide the answers.

Author's Tip

Within holistic circles there is a common saying of 'being centered'. This basically means being present with yourself and the moments that arise naturally.

There are many duties to undertake on a daily basis, some of which are in the hands of other people, so we have no control over what can happen. As a result, the energy of life can easily become chaotic.

Our natural world does not conform to rules and regulations so it is easy to find ourselves floating around in the sea of life trying to make the best of what influences we do have. The beauty of Qigong is that every time you practise, you are constantly returning to centre, always able to return to the present moment.

This method of gathering your energy allows you to sail a calm and steady course when the world around you proves to be less than harmonious. As your practice develops you also become more aware of how you feel when you are out of balance and sometimes you can even 'see' chaos before it happens.

Through daily practise this sense of feeling grows within you and enables you to recognise the signs and navigate the obstacles that may take their toll on your health. I like to think of Qigong as a great set of tools that we can use to take better care of our health and make positive steps to ensure your health doesn't suffer.

Although our ailments and illnesses can sometimes consume us and feel larger than life, you must remember there is always a solution if you keep things simple and put your intention in the right place.

If you are determined to get better, to relieve that ache or injury, then it's far more likely to work than if you relied on hope or changes to your circumstances. You already have the answers to many questions; you just need to want to act on them.

As the core purpose of this book is to provide each student with a solid foundation for future Qigong practise, I will not dwell on the deeper relationships of physical and emotional illness. It's such an interesting subject, and one I feel deserves a volume of its own.

For now, let's just get practising this wonderful art of health preservation and self-healing.

Chapter Two

Pure Organic Energy

The Most Powerful Source of Energy

The Power of the Organs

One of the major goals of Qigong practise is to maintain the health and function of the internal organ systems.

Each organ has a specific role to play to keep us alive with every breath we take. When illness and injury occur, our amazing bodies and minds get to work fixing and restoring our health, constantly adjusting the balance to return us to a point of equilibrium, free of illness and pain.

Traditional Chinese Medicine (TCM) categorises changes to health in two groups. We have external illnesses that may have been caused by an external factor such as physical traumas from accidents and injuries, an infectious disease that has invaded the body system, or a reaction to climatic changes like heat, cold, damp and wind. These are generally forces that come from the outside to affect the inside.

The other group is internal illnesses. These are symptoms and illnesses that result from imbalances on the inside of the body, our organ system.

Internal illnesses are usually a result of an external injury, such as feeling sick after eating poor-quality food, experiencing the stress and pain of a broken bone, or in most cases, the effect that we have when our emotions have been injured or shaken.

We all know how poor our health can be when we lose someone we love. The grief and sadness can weaken our immunity and willpower which often results in recurring colds and viruses.

Sedentary lifestyles can cause the joints and muscles to ache through lack of movement or for many of us we may have an unknown chronic illness that gradually seeps into our health changing our lives forever. These are symptoms of an internal imbalance from an external force.

Whether the imbalance has come from and internal or external force, all illnesses and injuries will cause a change in the way the body uses and distributes energy to help restore our health.

If you are strong during these periods, then the body and mind will recover and you will return to a normal level of health. If the body and mind are weak, then it will take more time and patience to recover. As we age, our energy levels naturally begin to decline, so recovering from ill health and injuries takes a little longer.

Or at least that is what most people think!

One of the great things I have experienced myself and seen in students is the restoration of youthfulness through the gentle practise of Qigong. Feeling old and the number of years you have been alive, have only a small part to play in how you actually 'feel'.

If the health of your body and mind is a direct result of the health of your energy system, then it makes sense that when the energy inside you is fresh, nourished and cultivated regularly, there is nothing to say you won't feel that way too!

I was always amazed at how youthful my Qigong teachers seemed. It was like talk-ing with teenagers, but they were in their sixties and seventies!

Over the years I have seen this in students too. As the energy grows, so do the smiles on their faces. It's as if someone has removed a dark damp towel from their heads or pulled their feet from being stuck in the mud. As a teacher this is wonderful to see.

Later in the book you will see that I have included some stories from students so that you can read how they feel about Qigong and how it has changed their lives.

In a nutshell, the practise of Qigong primarily helps to keep the energy system moving freely and the organs functioning correctly so that all parts of the body and mind are nourished and able to complete the many duties that are required.

To make this even more simple…

Qigong = Good Health.

And for good health we need good energy, so let's learn a little about how our energy system works.

Switching on the System

To begin building an idea of how the energy system works, let's look at some simple ways we can understand how energy moves around the body.

Perhaps you have heard of the word 'Qi' (pronounced 'chi') commonly used to describe our 'life force' by those that practise the methods of healing or alternative medicine.

New students are always curious about what Qi is and how it works. A common way to explain this is to compare Qi to electricity or a magnetic presence. The energy system of pathways compares to an electrical circuit board. As most people are aware of how electricity works, this seems like a very good place to start.

There are twelve main energy channels within the body system, each related to a specific organ on its path. These channels are commonly known as 'meridians', but for the purpose of this book, I will refer to them as pathways or vessels as the word 'meridian' does not convey the quality or magnitude of this amazing network.

Each of the twelve vessels has a 'yang' (active) and a 'yin' (storing) function. They also relate to the five elements of nature: Metal, Water, Wood, Fire and Earth. They are paired according to their function and element.

The Twelve Main Vessels

- Lungs and large Intestines – Metal
- Liver and gall bladder - Wood
- Heart and small intestines - Fire
- Stomach and spleen - Earth
- Kidney and bladder - Water
- Ren and Du (extra vessels)

The last two on our list; known as the Ren (conception vessel) and Du (governing vessel) are paired due to their relationship and formation while we grow in our mother's womb. Together they help to regulate the ten main energy vessels, keeping everything running nice and smooth.

As most of the symptoms we experience during illness and injury are related and treatable via the ten main pathways, that is where we will stay with this book.

So, let's move on and learn about the individual organs and how our energy system really works.

The Organ System

Each organ has its own function or job to do within the body and many rely on the functions of each other to work efficiently.

In TCM, all illness is a result of an imbalance of Qi, or sickness in the organ system which affects the way our energy moves around the body.

The energy of the organ system passes through a constant daily cycle over 24 hours, (*Fig 2.1*) beginning with the lungs in the early morning and passing through a two-hour cycle or phase over the course of the 24 hours.

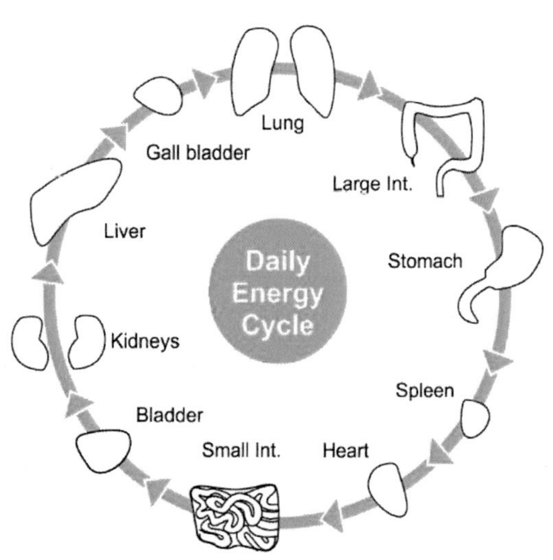

Fig 2.1

Two-Hour Cycles

- Lungs 3am-5am
- Large Intestine 5am-7am
- Stomach 7am-9am
- Spleen 9am-11am
- Heart 11am-1pm
- Small Intestine 1pm-3pm
- Bladder 3pm-5pm
- Kidneys 5pm-7pm
- Pericardium 7pm-9pm
- Triple Warmer 9pm-11pm
- Gall bladder 11pm-1am
- Liver 1am-3am

We call this energy cycle a biorhythm. There will be more about this in a later chapter.

As you can see from the two-hour cycle list, each organ has a specific time in the 24-hour day when it performs its duty and functions to maintain balance.

The anatomical illustration (*Fig 2.2*) will give you an idea of the organ placement within the body.

During the daily energy cycle, the level of activity and the overall health of each organ depends entirely on how we live our lives and what our lifestyle is like.

Each person's energy or blueprint is unique to them, so there is no better or worse design, just good or bad Qi circulation. Some of us may have inherited a weakness in a specific organ or perhaps our organs have been injured through misuse or injury.

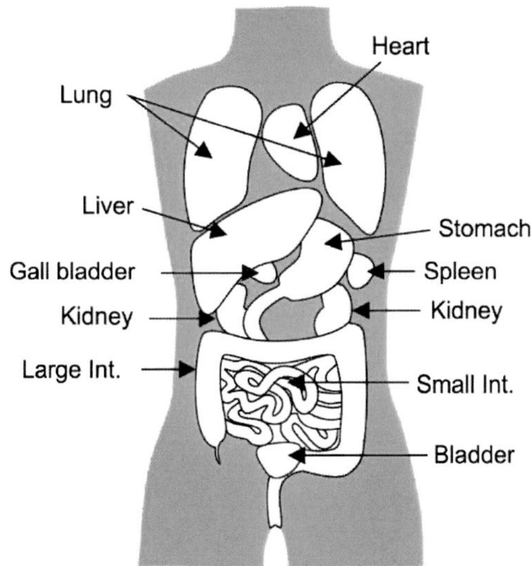

Fig 2.2

If you smoke, you may have a weakness of the lungs. If your diet is poor, you may have a weakness of the digestive organs. Prolonged stress may affect the heart or perhaps you have an infection or disease that causes damage.

The variables of health are endless. Life is different for each and every one of us and the personal health journey is also a very individual experience indeed! Even though our individual journeys are different, there is always a way to improve our health and well-being. Some of us have physical disabilities, some of us have emotional disabilities. We must make the best of what we have to work with.

When we practise Qigong, we are actively using a variety of methods to maintain and regulate the energy in the body so that the organs can function correctly. When one organ loses its ability to function efficiently it becomes the job of the other organs to step up and maintain the balance.

The Energy Generators

If we were to think of each organ as a mini generator or battery, where each organ has its own power but collectively they complete the energy circuit through the body, then we can begin to see what happens when organs become deficient in their healthy power or overloaded.

When this happens our ability to function normally is impaired causing our health to deteriorate and lack the vitality we feel when we are in good health. Looking at the diagram of the Daily Energy Circuit (*Fig 2.3*), let's say that each organ runs at its most optimum function at a level of five.

Throughout the 24-hour cycle, this may fluctuate a little higher or lower, but it generally stays around the midline between one (low) and ten (high).

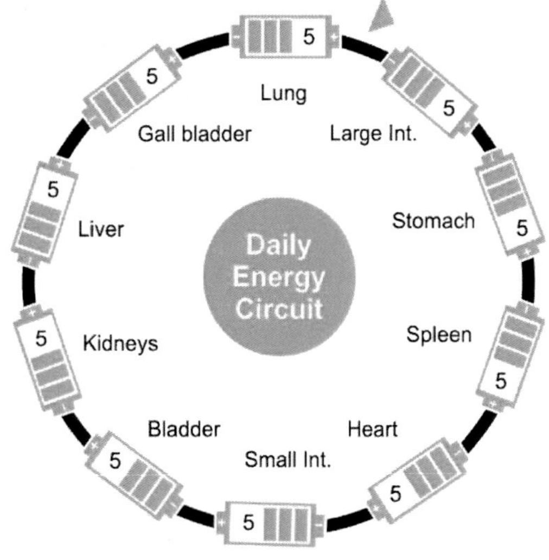

Fig 2.3

For this example (and to provide a very rough idea), I am going to suggest that when the power becomes low, we would feel fatigue, with a lowered immune system and our mood would be low, and we may feel sluggish. When the power is high, we can become anxious, angry, we are unable to sleep and may experience excessive pain in the body.

These are very general assertions, but they illustrate the extreme possibilities well. Since there are many variations of how symptoms may present themselves for each illness or injury and as this book's focus is to provide you with tools to start your Qigong journey, I won't include any further discussion of the medical or diagnostic side of TCM in this volume. Perhaps it will be the subject of another of my books.

So, let's imagine that each of our organs is happy and generating a healthy level of power. The circuit is running nice and smooth and the result is we are in good health and feel well.

Now let's imagine you have a virus that unfortunately causes you to vomit. Immediately your stomach energy would be weakened. As your stomach energy is weakened, its power drains and is unable to provide the correct supply of power to the spleen, the next organ in the energy circuit. The result is the spleen begins to suffer and it becomes less efficient in its own function.

The spleen in TCM is responsible for our appetite and energy, so we will easily lose our desire to eat and feel exhausted.

Due to this loss of power of the stomach's energy supply, there is an additional knock-on effect. Not only does any imbalance in the circuit affect the next phase but it also begins to draw energy from the preceding power source.

In this case the stomach has become so weak it now drains the previous power source, the large intestine, by stealing power from it so that it can restore its own functionality levels. (*Fig 2.4*)

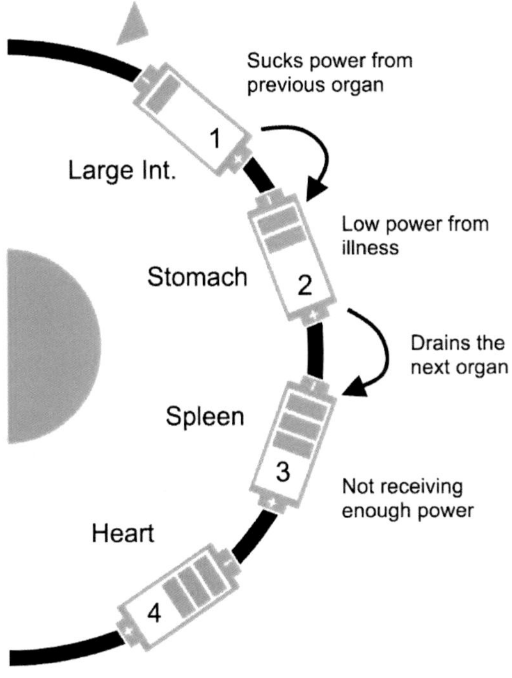

Fig 2.4

As a consequence, the large intestine now weakens. It no longer has the most efficient level of power to perform its own functions of removing water from the bowels and eliminating waste.

If the water is not removed from the bowel, we can have watery stools and diarrhoea. Coupled with the weakened bowel system, it's now more than likely that diarrhoea will follow.

So, as you can see in the diagram (*Fig 2.4*), the entire power system has been disrupted and thrown out of harmony. First, the stomach is disrupted by the vomiting. Due to its weakness, we lose our appetite and feel exhausted. The stomach draws energy from the large intestine and weakens its ability to maintain fluids in the bowel, so we have diarrhoea. All the components of a common virus!

For this example, we could suggest that the cause is an invasion of bacteria or even poison. To counter this, the body will rid itself of the intruder or we may need medicine to kill it, but it's the knock-on effect that also needs treatment and that is where Qigong steps in, to restore the balance of nature and harmony. Beautiful!

Although this is a very simplified or diluted explanation, the aim is to give you an 'idea' that your health and body function by means of a series of connected components.

Imagine a bicycle chain with each link connecting to the next to ensure a smooth and trouble-free bike ride. When one link fails, the bike will falter and we may fall off.

Similarly, when one of our body components fails, it can affect the others too and a pattern of various illnesses can be the result.

Each time you practise Qigong you are restoring those connections by regulating your whole body and mind, balancing them and correcting any disturbance to maintain the natural flow.

When you begin to see that there is always a pattern to how illness is initiated, you start to understand just how important it is to take action and not ignore any signs or signals you have.

The virus example is a relatively common occurrence. We are more than equipped to deal with its strain on the body but imagine if you already have a weakness that you have ignored and your power is already too low. What happens when your energy circuit really begins to suffer?

With regular practise, Qigong helps to repair and restore the power in your body, maintains the natural flow of the organ functions and reduces the chances of illness, disease and injuries, and we'd all like a bit of that!

Author's Tip

Many years ago, I picked up a virus on holiday abroad. I suffered with sickness and diarrhoea for weeks. I lost 16 lbs/7 kg in the first four weeks and my clothes were falling off my body.

I developed intolerances to milk, wheat and spicy foods. I felt like I had a permanent hangover. I was constantly fatigued, sleeping most afternoons when I could and life had become very depressing.

At this point I had been practising Qigong intermittently for a few years. My health was what I would call 'pretty good'. This illness was a great wake-up call and also an historical turning point in my Qigong journey.

I began to focus more on studying Qigong, developing a regular routine, investing my spare money in further tuition and letting go of many things in my life to make room for improving my health. I resolved never to feel that way again.

It took around three years of being mindful of my health and incorporating a regular Qigong session into my life to recover properly.

The results are that I no longer have food intolerances or extended periods of fatigue.

There was a time, like for most people, when it would take many days to recover from an illness and injuries would linger for weeks before healing. This is not so now. Many of my students remark at how well and quickly they recover from illness or injuries too! That's if they get ill at all.

It rarely happens when you have an everyday Qigong in your life!

Author's Extra Tip

Throughout the book I have provided some space for you to make notes of your experience as you progress through the pages.

Please use these pages to record your thoughts, feelings and ideas. You can even draw pictures if you like! I do. There's one coming up soon so get your pen or pencil ready to jot something down.

Now, let's take a quick look at how the emotions can affect our health and the organs.

Emotions and the Organs

In terms of TCM, each of the organs is affected by certain emotions and is associated with a specific body part. Each organ is also linked to its own particular element.

The following table (*Fig 2.5*) shows the relationship between the organ system, specific parts of the body, the five elements of nature, and our range of emotions. It illustrates how an imbalance can result in illness or symptoms of illness in its associated body part and the likely emotion experienced as a result.

Similarly, an organ imbalance can produce particular emotions or physical symptoms in its related body parts. As an example, if the kidney energies are low, then you might feel the emotion of fear or apprehension. This fear can range from very mild to very strong feelings of anxiety depending on the duration or strength of the imbalance.

With stress, which is a complaint commonly affecting the liver energies, a person may feel tightness in the joints and possibly suffer with tendon problems. They may also be short-tempered and display outbursts of anger.

In many cases, more than one organ system will be affected, so multiple body parts can produce different problems. This is where traditional diagnosis of the whole body and mind really shines through. I would recommend a TCM diagnosis to anyone with multiple symptoms or chronic illness.

The table shown (*Fig 2.5*) is very general and forms only a small part of how TCM uses various relationships and patterns to make an overall diagnosis about your health.

Later you will discover how the Qigong movements detailed in this book relate to each organ system and how they can be used to bring balance and harmony to your state of general well-being. The table will give you a basic idea of which body parts and emotions are related to each organ.

I like to think of the emotions as the way that the organs communicate with the mind to let you know something needs attention. Emotions are the physical voice of healing. Over time, through the practise of Qigong, you will learn to listen more attentively and take action to prevent ill health.

ORGAN	ELEMENT	BODY	EMOTION
LUNGS & LARGE INTESTINE	METAL	SKIN	SADNESS GRIEF
KIDNEYS & BLADDER	WATER	BONES	FEAR APPREHENSION
LIVER & GALL BLADDER	WOOD	TENDONS	ANGER FRUSTRATION
HEART & SMALL INTESTINES	FIRE	BLOOD VESSELS	JOY EXCITEMENT
STOMACH & SPLEEN	EARTH	MUSCLES	WORRY PENSIVENESS

Fig 2.5 Organs, Emotions and Body Parts

The Organ Biorhythm

Throughout the day, the cycle of energy passes through the organ system. In TCM this can be used as a diagnosis tool to understand how the energy of the body and mind are reacting at certain times and what state the energy of the organ is in at that specific time phase.

Symptoms that appear at various daily times can be a great clue to a practitioner of TCM regarding the health of the patient. As the energy cycles through its path the vessels are activated providing insight into the present state of the organ system and the symptoms that may give an indication as to the health of the patient.

You can also see (*Fig 2.6*) that there are times throughout the day that are more suited to certain activities than others.

Having a bowel movement first thing in the morning, 5am to 7am as the large intestine (colon) is active. Eating breakfast between 7am and 9am because the stomach energy is moving through its cycle. Staying calm between 11am and 1pm will help the emotional heart.

During the night-time you can see that the cycle passes through the gall bladder, liver and lungs. These organs deal with detoxifying the body so resting during these periods is very beneficial.

Lack of rest and sleep during these cycles like: late night-shift working and insomnia could eventually weaken these organ systems and cause imbalances.

These are just general ideas, but it will give you a basic understanding how the cycle functions.

Biorhythms is a subject in which I have a great interest and I hope to publish more on this topic one day, but for now, let's discover the three things everybody wants.

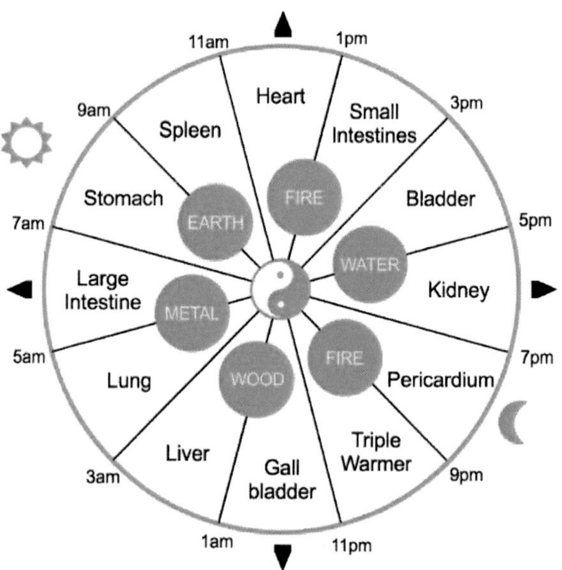

Fig 2.6

Student Notes

Chapter Three

The Three Things Everybody Wants!

The Simple Solutions

Regaining Your Youth

During my years of teaching Qigong, treating patients and meeting many different students, there have been three very basic goals that most people aspire to in order to enjoy a full and vibrant journey through life:

1. To feel less stress
2. To have less pain
3. To have the energy to enjoy life

I can assure you, from my own personal experience and from the results my students have reported, Qigong will help you achieve all three of these goals!

Let me tell you how…

Qigong is very simple, and like most things, you get out of it what you put in. For me personally Qigong has become my daily medicine and I find this a great way to think about it too.

For those of you who find yourselves with aches and pains here and there, Qigong will help you to relax and relieve stiff muscles and achy joints. The results can be immediate and a daily practice will help keep you in tip top condition.

If you are unfortunate enough to have a chronic condition that has troubled you for many years, it will obviously take a little longer before you notice an im-provement.

This of course means you'll have more time enjoying your Qigong session and really getting to know how your health clock ticks. You may also begin to un-derstand how your journey has unfolded so far, so stick with it and you'll really notice the results and feel the benefits in no time at all. In all its essence, Qigong can be a simple health maintenance system or a journey of self-discovery and transformation. It really does suit everyone.

As we get older, many of us can feel our youthfulness ebbing away as we take on more and more physical and mental duties on a daily basis. Fatigue and tiredness are two of the most common symptoms experienced as we age and we'd all like some more energy, wouldn't we?

One of the greatest aspects of Qigong is that through this simple and effective practice, you can regain that sense of youthfulness and restore that spark of life that we all feel radiated so much brighter in our younger years.

The other basic need we all have is less stress. That feeling of being overloaded with duties or thoughts can make life a very frantic experience. When it comes to emotional stress and feelings of tension, Qigong can be a daily remedy, a gift to yourself and a much-needed moment of peace and tranquillity.

Through regular daily practise, the physical body gradually begins to relax and release the tension we have accumulated over the years. For many of us, this means less pain and fewer annoying niggles we feel in our body.

When the aches and pains subside, there is less 'mental noise' to deal with, that shoulder no longer screams for you to stop lifting it or that nagging in your knee telling you to stop walking quietly fades away. You have provided space for the mind to be quiet and the emotions begin to relax and calm down.

Over time, the mind begins to unwind and you can see things more clearly. The little-and-often annoying, trivial irritations dissolve, leaving just the meaningful thoughts for you to ponder over and resolve or just let go of, leaving opportunities for you to replenish other areas of your life. Eventually you will recognise those aspects of your life which are genuinely causing you to feel unhappy. Then you can take action to heal and restore personal health.

Having a clearer picture of what is making you unhappy can help you to make gradual and positive changes that lift the burdens of stress and allow many problems to be resolved naturally.

For many, health has become a constant struggle, an up-hill climb with no sight of the mountain peak. When days are like this, it's very easy to give up and seek easier routes to wellness, such as medications, satisfying food cravings or other substitutes which you think will make you feel better.

I have always felt that healing should be a natural process and not a battle or a fight! I feel those that are encouraged to fight illness or 'beat' their symptoms only add to the stress and heartache, draining much needed resources.

Once the emotional burdens have lifted, the fog clears from the mind and the heaviness of the limbs dissipates. This will provide you with space to restore energy, relieve stress so you can return to a happier, more enjoyable life.

It really can be that simple, but I also understand that it may seem very hard for new students in the beginning. It was for me too, but look at me now, I'm writing a book about it!

So, let's take a look at what Qigong is and how it will help you reach these goals.

Your Daily Medicine

Qigong comes in many forms and guises. There are countless styles and even many variations of those styles. There are Qigong systems for development of the physical body, systems to cultivate the spiritual self, religious systems and many others aimed at specific diseases.

The system I am going to share with you in this book is aimed at our three main goals.

1. Less Stress

2. Less Pain

3. More Energy

On the outside, to those who are not familiar with Qigong, it is very common to see it as a slow-moving exercise system, which in some respects it is. Some will think it is Tai Chi (martial art system) as this has become more popular over the years and its slow movements are very similar.

Over the past decade I have seen more and more doctors and health workers recommend Tai Chi to patients. This is an amazing step forward in movement therapies, but there is still a huge lack of knowledge by these professionals.

Although Taijiquan (Tai Chi) 'practise' can be very beneficial, it is predominantly a combat fighting system. I remember my first Taiji teacher always said 'Taiji is a devastating fighting system *with* health benefits'. Those that have trained Taiji will know this too.

In terms of health, Tai Chi has many benefits, but it is not specifically a health system like Qigong. For this reason, I feel that those that seek greater health with Tai Chi are better off investing precious time in Qigong, or better still, try both together.

Tai Chi helps to move the energy through the vessels which will improve your health but it does not specifically regulate the system like Qigong as this is not the primary goal of Tai Chi.

Our goal in Qigong is to regulate the energy pathways through specific practices to harmonise and strengthen the entire functions and processes of the body and mind. To instil balance in the ever-changing ecosystem of our bodies so that we can better enjoy the full breath of life.

With this renewed health and practise of regulating energy comes many benefits, one of which is that it helps to improve everything else you do in your life at the same time. Whether you train in martial arts, gymnastics, football or roller-skating, the methods in this book will help make these activities feel more enjoyable because you will feel more relaxed, more energetic and able to recover quicker!

It's not only the physical activities either. Maybe you're the best business manager, social worker, hairdresser or even a deep-sea diver, the holistic benefits of Qigong will radiate in everything you do in life.

For me, it helps to keep my arms and shoulders relaxed when I play my guitar for long periods (at least when I find time to play it). It makes my job as a body-worker and healer more enjoyable and intuitive. I even found my creative and artistic side has grown a lot.

When I find time to do some drawing or artwork, I'm never short of inspiration. In fact, I even felt inspired enough to design all the illustrations in this book from photos of myself and my wife (yes, that's really me and my wife in all the pictures!).

I'll admit I hated being in front of the computer and my back ached after every drawing, but I absolutely loved it and the aches and pains just encouraged me to do more Qigong! How great is that?

It's not just about being physically and mentally healthy, it's about being whole. Feeling connected and nourishing everything that you are, body, mind and soul, and that's just what you need to make this life journey feel better.

So, let's look at what 'regulating' means and how it affects our ecosystem of health.

Regulation of Health

When illness and injury occur, our personal ecosystem is often thrown out of balance and we begin to experience symptoms related to whichever part of the body or emotions that are affected.

The body now begins to gather its resources and release stored energy to help rebalance the functions, heal what needs healing and return to a harmonious state that we all feel is 'good health'.

In most cases the body and mind are amazing at doing this job especially when we are younger and our energy systems have not been damaged by life's trials and traumas. As we age, this process begins to slow down so our illnesses and injuries take a little longer to heal. This is a natural process and one which should be embraced and nurtured. Many of us will find ageing troublesome and fall into the trap of accepting that life is a downward slope.

Maybe you have stopped doing the physical things you used to love because they now cause you pain or an injury has left you restricted and you have decided to take the 'safe' road from now on.

Emotional restrictions are becoming more common too. Anxieties, depression, low self-esteem and personal confidence are now the new illnesses that keep us contained and disconnected from life's magical moments.

There are endless circumstances in life that keep us from the life we desire, but this need not be when you have Qigong in your life.

We all get low sometimes and our immune systems are constantly tested, so what we all need is a little something that makes a BIG difference!

Over time and with regular daily practise the aches diminish, emotions begin to calm and there is less debris for the body and mind to deal with. This allows both to return to a normal healthy state much more easily and quickly.

As the body and mind become more efficient, like a fine-tuned sports car or musical instrument, we find that illness no longer lingers for long and the aches and pains are less noticeable or in many cases completely resolved, much like it was when we were in our youth.

You can think of it as giving yourself a helping hand to get better each and every day, just like creating your own daily dose of medicine. For those that dedicate themselves to a regular practice you will begin to see Qigong in every moment of life.

All you have to do is decide what you want to do with your time here. Are you currently enjoying your life? Could you make changes to improve daily health? Or do you feel like you need a little help?

It doesn't matter whether you are 18 or 80, there is a very strong chance that investing some of your time into the practice of Qigong could bring you a brighter, better life.

Author's Tip

I spend a lot of my time in clinic treating elderly patients that excel in their lives because they know how precious time is, but why wait until you are in your later years to invest? Start saving now in the 'bank of health' and enjoy the benefits you have gained today!

Investing in health should be like taking a long, slow ride on the bike of life … as long as you keep pedalling you will see the brightness of life, feel the sun on your face and the wind through your hair. The benefits can be priceless.

Take your time, learn, study, talk to those that know and really enjoy the process of creating your own health journey. Talk to your doctor, meet with therapists, try new foods, get a massage, take a soak in a warm bath, go for a walk, and remember to smile often.

Get your friends, family, children and loved ones involved too, practise together and make it a time for play.

Most important of all, HAVE FUN!

Learning is so much easier when you are having fun. It's a major factor for me when I think about health and I hope at this point you are feeling confident and ready to get things moving with your physical practise of Qigong.

In the next chapter we will begin our first practical exercise, 'Finding Your Centre', but before we do I wanted to share a story with you that really helped me get a 'feeling' of the magic of Qi

The Health Dynamo

When it comes to TCM, there are four pillars or branches: Acupuncture; Tui Na Massage; Medical Qigong; and Herbs. This forms a complete internal and external system of medicine. It's a big subject that can be confusing to those new to holistic medicine, especially when it comes to the subject of Qi (Chi).

There is always great difficulty in translating the Chinese language into others and quite often, some of the meaning is lost. The word Qi is no exception and one that can be easily misunderstood.

Most simplified explanations are 'life force', 'life energy', 'breath' or in some cases 'an invisible force that moves around the body'. In some ways these are correct but in other ways they only touch the surface of the meaning of Qi.

For me, I like to think of Qi as 'activity', a sense of life, action or of something that has a quality or potential. When a flower opens in the morning sun you can see the energy of life growing before your eyes as it changes from a sleepy bud into an array of colour and attraction. This is the beauty of Qi at work and a great example of the process of change and action.

In this book we are going to promote and develop our human Qi or energy that relates to our body and mind. These are the functions and processes of our blood, fluids, organs, muscles, bones, tendons, tissues and the emotional representation of Qi.

One of the ways that I use to explain what we are trying to achieve with the practise of Qigong is the 'dynamo effect'. This is a series of components and movements united together to produce a specific result, in this case, light.

My Shiny Silver Light

When I was a child I had a very smart silver bike and I remember the day I got my first light for that bike. Having it meant I could stay out a little later to play with my friends in the street.

The light was large, shiny, silver in finish and sat on top of my handle bars. From the back of the light ran a long cable that travelled along the top of the bike frame and down to the back wheel.

On the back of the bike frame near the rear wheel my dad fitted what looked like a small, solid silver bottle with a black plastic top on the end. As a young seven-year old, I was very intrigued!

After the clamps were secured and the cable fitted, I excitedly looked for a switch to turn the light on, but there was no switch or button in sight. I was heart-broken when the light didn't work, there was no switch and I couldn't find a way to get it working! Then I heard a CLUNK! on the back wheel and my dad said, 'ride it!'.

I got on my bike and began to pedal. As I pedalled away from my dad, the light began to shine, dimly at first, but it shone nonetheless. I was chuffed, but very bemused too, so I had to investigate more.

With a dynamo system, when you needed to use the light you had to push the rear silver bottle onto the tyre so the top, which I now saw was a small ribbed cog, was touching the tyre.

When the tyre rotated, it would turn the plastic cog, which in turn generated an electric current inside the silver bottle, sending it along the cable and the light would come on. I was amazed! I didn't hang around to ask any questions either! I just rode that bike as much as I could, trying to light everything in my path.

The thing that I'll always remember about that bike is that when I pedalled slowly the light was very dim and didn't emit enough light to see where I was going.

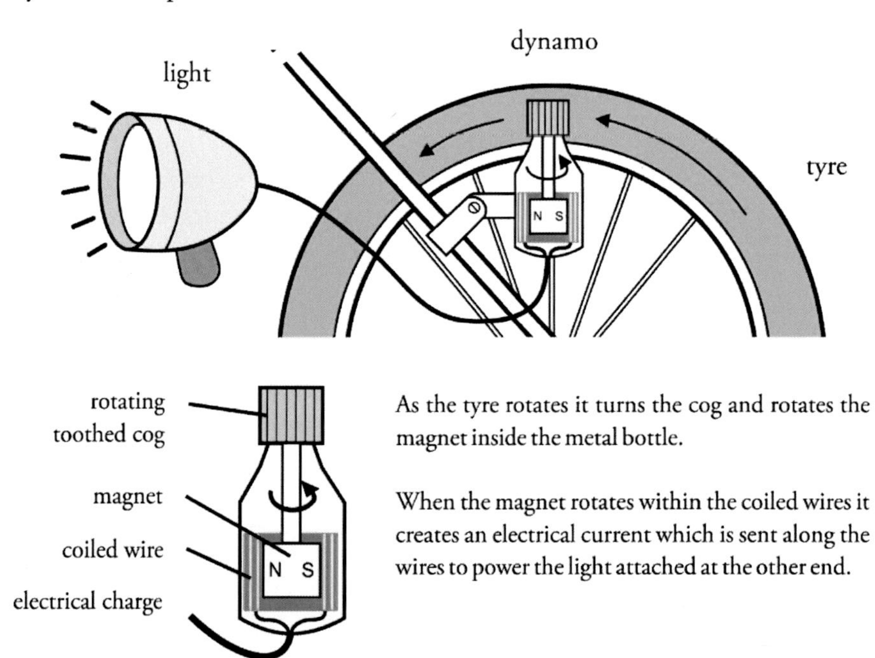

When I pedalled as hard as I could, the light would be as bright as it could be, until one day the bulb blew.

Downhill was always easiest! And anyone who had a dynamo on their bike back then knew as soon as you pushed the dynamo to the tyre, that bike became a lot harder to pedal! The trouble is, you can't go downhill forever, sooner or later you must climb that hill to get back to the top.

My dad replaced the bulb and told me to go steady next time, so I did. I pedalled at a good, even pace and the light shone enough for me to see my way in the dark. One very happy seven-year old, but with very tired legs! Phew!

When I came to Chinese medicine and the study of Qigong, this experience as a child resonated with my practice and the process of energy production.

You see, all you have to do is keep the light working, nice and steady and it will light the way for you. Pedal through life too hard and there is a good chance your bulb will blow, or you'll run out of energy to emit even the slightest light.

On the other hand, if you don't put enough effort into turning the wheel, the light will be too dim and there will be no energy for the bulb to produce its light at all. This is often the case with illness. We lack the energy to physically move so we can generate the required activity to improve our health.

The practice of Qigong is much the same as the dynamo system I loved so much. If you just go steady, there will be enough Qi to enjoy life. It makes sense that if we want to have a long and vibrant life we just have to maintain a constant and relaxed amount of activity to light the journey.

A regular, gentle but daily nudge is all it takes to maintain good function and health. Some of you will need to step it up a bit and move more as lack of movement can cause many illnesses and especially pain. Others will need to slow down and find a middle ground to stop the racing mind and anxious body.

Qigong in all its simplicity will help you return to this steady centre time and time again. It's like the best friend anyone could have, always letting you know when to slow down to rest and restore or increase your activity to light the journey of life.

Be your own dynamo and let the light of health shine through!

The Greatest Gift!

By now you may have realised that I'm 'slightly' passionate about my Qigong! However, I do find that this love for Qigong and my journey to help others can sometimes seem slightly exaggerated when I talk about it to new students.

I often catch myself sounding like a salesman for Qigong, but as my training develops, my health improves and there have been changes that doctors could never have brought about.

Over the years I have realised, you cannot put Qigong into a box as there is no way to understand or verbally explain what happens when the body begins to heal, other than to experience it for yourself, as every journey is different.

This book will provide you with the necessary tools and information to get you started in the right direction. The rest is up to you. So, without further ado, (ta da) my last 'pitch' will be this:

Author's Final Pitch (maybe)

Qigong ticks a lot of boxes! At the time when I found Qigong I needed something to keep me physically healthy. I also needed stress relief and more energy, and boy did I get it, and much, much more! Now it's your turn, to get what you need. This is my gift to you.

If you are now ready, let's get started with our first exercise to help find our centre of health and balance.

Student Notes

Qigong is not a race!

There are no quick ways to move through the stages of healing.

All you have to do is practise.

Let Nature take its course and enjoy the view.

It's such a lovely journey.

Chapter Four

The First Step is the Greatest

'A journey of a thousand miles
begins with just one small step'

Lao Tzu

Finding Your Centre

Finding your centre is an amazing tool when creating a balanced life experience. When the world around us becomes chaotic or our daily lives take unexpected turns, we all need to be able to gather ourselves and our emotions. When we centre ourselves, we are continuously be-coming aware of both our physical and emotional health.

Centring involves building awareness of your physical body, reconnecting your mind to your body and learning to release restrictions that can reduce the overall functions of good health.

This process is like having a healthy spring clean every day, even many times per day to maintain our focus and enjoy our everyday lives. Once you learn how to centre your mind and body it can be as simple as just one deep and attentive breath. Perfect!

At the beginning of our Qigong practise, we start by gathering our thoughts, connecting to our breath and surrendering our body to the support of the earth. We are learning to become still, like gently calming the unsettled ocean waves into the gentle flow of a woodland stream.

With each of the following postures, we stimulate and calm the inner vessels of the energy system. Then we use the physical body and movements to circulate the Qi around the body. This helps to nourish the bones, muscles, tissues and every cell that keeps us alive and happy.

It can be like placing a hand into a stream and unsettling the waterbed. This allows the stream to transport the dirt and debris away with its natural flow of direction and intent.

After we have cleared one stream, we return to centre, allowing the waterbed to settle and the water to run clear. Once we have cleared and settled, we can move on to the next posture, or energy stream.

This gentle process of attention to self, or rather, self-attention, is what helps to grow our Qigong practice.

Take your time, there is no rush, become still and all will follow naturally.

Here is your first practise exercise.

The Ten Checkpoints

To begin, stand with the feet shoulder-width apart, placing the hands on top of each other just below the navel. Then gently move through the following check-points.

1. **Suspend the head.** Feel as if the crown of the head is gently suspended by a thread to the sky. Breathe in and out.

2. **Relax your mind.** I always find visualizing a cloudy sky in my mind and then breathe in. As I breathe out, I see the clouds drift apart and the light of the sun shine through.

3. **Relax the shoulders.** Take your attention to your neck and the area that runs outwards to the shoulder joints. Gently breathe inwards and let the breath travel to the tension like inflating a balloon around the area. Then breathe out allowing the balloon to deflate taking with it the discomforts and unease as the tension pours down the arms towards the hands.

4. **Relax the chest.** Take a slow and relaxed breath inward, allowing the chest, back and abdomen to expand outwards. Slowly release the breath and relax.

5. **Relax the elbows.** Breathe into the elbows and as you breathe out allow the joint to soften and the tension to seep downward towards the wrists. Slowly release the hands and let them fall naturally to the sides of the body.

6. **Breathe into the wrists.** Allow them to expand like a small balloon. Breathe out as the balloons deflate and allow the tension to run downwards out of the finger tips, falling to the floor.

7. **Release the hips.** Gently breathe into the hips, sides of the legs and buttocks. As you breathe out allow any tension to pour downward around the legs and into the earth below. Allow the weight of the body to relax into the feet.

8. **Relax the knees.** Breathe into the knees as if inflating two small balloons. Breathe out allowing them to slowly melt away and fall towards the floor.

9. **Relax the feet.** Allow the soles of the feet to gently spread into the floor. Breathe in gently. As you breathe out allow the body to slowly sink through all the checkpoints gradually releasing any tension through the feet and into the earth.

10. **Return to centre.** Slowly place the hands back to the area of the navel and breathe gently for ten breaths.

If you feel emotional or tense at this point you can simply repeat the process again, the next time is always better! For some students it takes time to relax. We all have different bodies and ailments so enjoy each section as you move through this book. Take it slowly one step at a time.

This process of relaxation can be used as a stand-alone routine on its own, at any time, to recover your thoughts and steady your mind. As you become better at your practice and your Qi starts to grow, the process of centring becomes second nature and you may even find yourself doing it without even realising it.

Imagine … training without training, getting healthy with every waking moment without realising it. Now that's medicine!

Try to practise this simple centring exercise everyday if you can. It really helps to reconnect your mind to the physical body which helps you to 'feel' your true state of health.

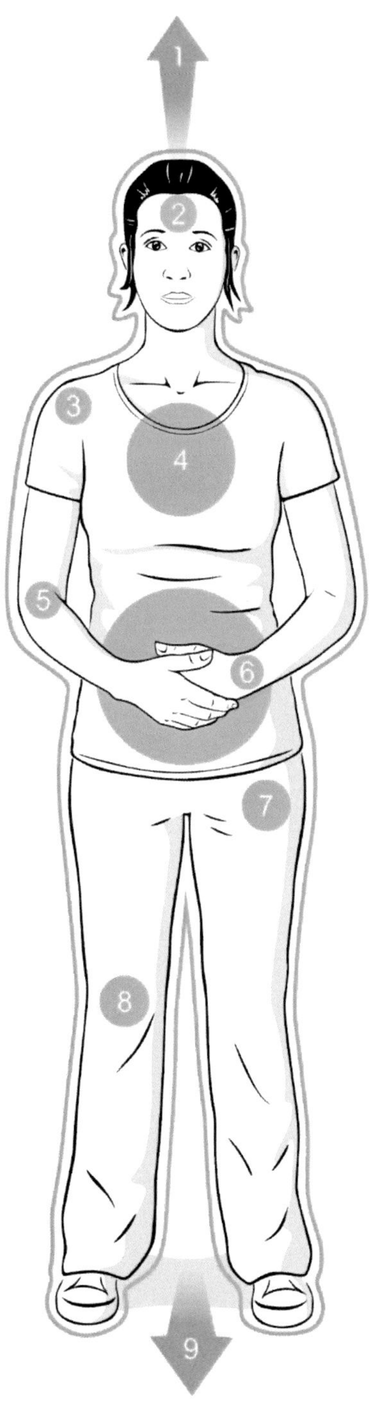

Chapter Five

The Beautiful, Magic You

Discovering Your Body

Basic Body Systems

Now that we have discussed the basic ideas of Qigong and connected our mind and body, it really helps to get an idea of what we are actually working with when we practise our Qigong for health.

Our first stop on the journey is learning about the physical body and its functions, so let's take a look at the basic body systems.

Respiration

When people think of respiration we think of breathing. Breathing is something we do automatically every minute of the day without giving it a second thought. This is the core need of many living things. For most people, as long as we are breathing we are generally okay, and we are all fully aware of how we feel when, for whatever reason, we can't breathe!

The word Qi is often translated into 'air' or 'breath', it is our connection to the external world, the very component that brings us life, but it is much more than that, it's what we do with the air inside the body that really makes a difference to health.

With each and every breath, we provide our bodies with oxygen, a gas that constitutes around 21% of the atmosphere on earth. For humans to exist, oxygen is needed to complete a process within the body that creates the very energy we need to function and feel alive.

With every breath, oxygen is taken into the lungs and transported to the blood system to be distributed around the body for its many uses. The principal function of this oxygen is to help produce energy from the food we eat.

Oxygen combines with glucose, a simple carbohydrate (simple sugar) found in the foods we eat, to create a chemical reaction. This reaction produces a usable form of energy known as Adenosine Triphosphate (ATP), which is a molecule that stores and transports chemical energy within our cells.

I like to think of ATP as the spark that lights the fire of life, or the very fuel of the human body.

The by-product of this process is a waste made up of carbon dioxide and water which is expelled from the body every time we breathe out.

The process of respiration is ultimately our source of energy or Qi derived from nutrition, so having a regular supply of the best foods combined with clean air and efficient breathing can quite literally make us feel alive, strong and energetic.

You can also begin to see that poor diet and foods low in nutritional value, such as processed foods, have a direct effect on how energetic we feel and how resistant our body is to illness.

Lack of movement and a lazy intake of oxygen will also reduce the effectiveness of our energy production. The respiratory process is also affected by the emotions. Grief and depression will make our breathing shallow and reduce our oxygen intake. Overexcitement, anxiety and fear can increase our breath rate so we become jittery, shaky and even manic.

This also works the other way too. Emotions like grief, loss, sadness, depression, anxiety, nervousness and anger can all be a result of a lack of correct respiration or poor food and lack of movement. This is why a good diet, regular exercise and relaxed breathing can relieve a whole host of common symptoms that are often treated with pharmaceutical medications.

The most common symptoms of poor respiration could be: fatigue; tiredness; muscle pains; depression; anxiety; and low immune response.

Muscles

Muscles help to move joints, maintain blood flow and assist with many of the functions of the body. Some even say the brain is a muscle!

- Approximately 50% of our body is made up of muscle tissue.
- There are over 700 named muscles in the human body.
- Cardiac muscles help maintain heart function and blood flow.
- Visceral muscles can be found in the arteries, stomach and intestines. They help move substances by contracting to gently push various substances through the organs.
- Skeletal muscles contract and relax to assist with all movements like speaking, breathing, walking and all physical activity.
- Muscles help to maintain our posture and structure.
- Muscles provide a physical barrier to protect our internal organs.

The muscular system is very important as it's often the first signs we experience when health begins to suffer. We all experience pain and injury in the muscles, not to mention the tension from stress and emotional pain. By maintaining a healthy muscular system, we will immediately feel much healthier and more alive.

Healthy muscles will also keep us moving and active in the things we like to do throughout life. So always keep your body moving no matter what if you want to stay youthful!

There is a very common saying that you may have heard. 'Move it or lose it!' which speaks volumes if you want to help your mind and body stay fit and healthy.

One of the most important factors of muscle health is to ensure correct functioning of the muscular system. The muscles require a sufficient supply of oxygen, and that means effective breathing and a healthy respiratory system.

Therefore, if you have aches, pains, twitches or cramps, why not sit for a while and practise some soft breathing?

Bones

You may know that you need a regular supply of calcium for strong bones, and our bones help us to move and complete everyday activities, but what else do bones do for us?

- Bones provide the framework that supports our muscles and other body tissues.
- They store important nutrients and minerals needed for everyday health.
- Bones produce blood cells to protect the body against disease.
- Our skull protects the brain and other bones provide a deeper level of physical protection for the internal organs.
- Bones help us to physically move so we can enjoy life every day.

Tendons

Tendons are a form of connective tissue that connect muscles to bones. At the end of each muscle the tissue becomes denser and more structured, forming into a strong binding material that inserts into the bone tissues to help our joints move by leveraging of the muscles.

Tendons are usually injured by overuse of the muscles or friction created by nearby bony structures. Repetitive use can cause inflammation and reduced movements in the joints of the area where the affected tendons connect.

Ligaments

Ligaments are similar to tendons but with hardly any blood supply. They connect bones to bones and are generally extremely strong in structure and framework. They are like layer upon layer of netting, forming a unified and tough material.

Ligaments are generally quite robust and most will only experience an injury when a joint or connected structure is forced past its range of movement or directly stretched beyond its reach by physical trauma.

Blood

For most of us, blood is just a red liquid that travels throughout our bodies in arteries and vessels. We know the heart is there to pump the blood around so we are aware that good heart health is a must!

We also know that when we bleed, we need to stop that bleeding or we may die. For many, this is enough and it's not given a second of thought more. But what else does blood do?

- Transports oxygen around the body.
- Carries nutrients and hormones around the body.
- Helps to get rid of waste products from the many processes that the functions of the body have to make on a daily basis.
- Blood regulates our Ph. level which helps keep our internal environment from being too acidic or too alkaline.
- Maintains our body temperature.
- Keeps the correct balance of water in each and every living cell.
- Protects our body against disease.
- Helps to supply the body with fluids and minerals to keep cells healthy.

As you can see, blood does amazing things for us. Maintaining the smooth flow of blood and reducing anything that may block this flow is of utmost importance.

Common ailments related to lack of blood flow can be:

- Tiredness & fatigue
- Low immune response
- Headaches
- Muscle pain
- Hormonal imbalances

Fluids

Fluids tend to be recognised as any other fluids in the body other than blood.

Fluids are the body's natural oils and transport systems derived from the foods we eat. They help to nourish and lubricate or moisten the following:

- Joints
- Brain
- Bones
- Hair
- Muscles
- Organs

Deficiencies and lack of fluids can cause the skin to dry, lips to crack, eyes to become irritated, tendons and tissues to bind. It's not just about staying hydrated with fluids, like getting your daily dose of spring water, it's more to do with the organ system being able to produce, eliminate, and transport fluids around the body.

Lymphatic System

The lymphatic system is very similar to our blood vessel systems. But unlike blood vessels that have the action of the heart to physically pump the blood throughout our body, the lymphatic system relies on movement of the muscles and joints.

Lymph fluid is a clear fluid that surrounds all the spaces in the body between the structures and cells. This fluid helps to pump waste products around the body to be recycled and used again or eliminated as waste. Lymph fluid is moved around the body in lymphatic vessels and either returned to the blood system or stored in small balloon like sacs called lymph nodes.

Each of these nodes is sited at major junctions and the parts of the body that move most. The neck, shoulders, armpit, chest, abdomen, hips and knees are prominent sites to improve lymphatic movement by gently squeezing the nodes with every move we make.

Each time we move these areas lymph fluid is pumped around the body so that it can replenish and remove waste. Therefore, when you are immobile and the lymph system is not moving as efficiently, you may begin to feel unwell.

Many people begin to suffer with complaints as they age and become less mobile. Physical massage is very important to combat age-related problems, along with assisted physical movements. Due to the gentle movements, and less of a need for muscle strength, Qigong is probably one of the most effective forms of healthcare for ageing students.

The lymphatic system also produces antibodies which build our immune system by defending us. Antibodies help to eradicate or kill off foreign invaders like bacteria and disease.

When you practise holistic methods like Qigong you are in fact building your own protection from illness and disease. This makes Qigong great for those with suppressed immune functions and autoimmune conditions.

A great Qigong master once said, 'Qigong activates your body's own medicine'. I couldn't have put it better myself!

Here are the basic functions of the lymphatic system.

- Helps to transport white blood cells around the body to eliminate disease.
- Transports nutrients to cells and bones.
- Helps to eliminate metabolic waste.
- Lymph fluid is filtered at the nodes for bacteria, cancer cells, and other potentially-threatening agents.
- The lymphatic system creates antibodies to defend and fight off infection and diseases.

As you can see, the lymphatic system is very important so I highly recommend, if you have time, to add this to a personal study list.

From this brief explanation you can see the easiest way to maintain a healthy lymphatic system is to physically move the body! Gentle movements of the neck, jaw, shoulders, elbows, waist, hips, knees and ankles can make a huge difference to your health. Luckily, Qigong covers everything you need for a healthy lymphatic system.

Myofascia - The Majestic Net!

In my years of study and clinical practise, no other body part has been as prominent and inspiring as the fascia system. It is the one single organ that connects every part of the body together as one!

Fascia reaches to all depths and surfaces of the body encompassing the organs, arteries, vessels, muscles, bones, tissues and the brain. Without fascia, we would just fall to the ground like a sack full of bones. Fascia is the glue that keeps our structure and framework together.

If you have ever cut a piece of animal meat, sometimes you can see a very thin layer of white tissue in between the fibrous sections of the main flesh, that is the fascia. Even onions have a layer similar to this so take a look next time you are preparing a meal, it's a fascinating substance.

Fascia is also the bearer of many aches, pains and illnesses. Restrictions or inflammation in the fascia system can cause a lot of problems, many of which are sensations of pain that are felt elsewhere in the body other than the actual site of the problem.

This causes a lot of confusion in diagnosing medical conditions because until recently, western medicine has not given much thought to the fascia system at all.

When the fascia net is affected by restrictions, injuries or inflammation, discomfort can manifest itself in many different symptoms. The most common are muscle pain, joint pain, headaches, digestive complaints and general feelings of malaise.

The fascia net must be pliable and remain able to move freely between the body structures for us to feel we are in good health. As with most tissues in the body the fascia requires a good supply of fluids, namely blood, but other fluids are also used by this network, so hydration and movement are essential remedies.

Some say that the fascia holds all of our past memories which would explain how trauma remains locked in the body. Many of us have heard that the stomach is the second brain in the body, but maybe there is a third, the fascia.

The thing that amazed me most when I began to study fascia is that there were already methods and systems available to keep this organ in good health: Qigong and Yoga.

These methods have been around for thousands of years maintaining the health of our myofascia long before people actually knew what it was. Eastern health practices have always led the way in holistic health due to their longevity of study.

Only now as they become more popular and medical doctors are seeking alternative treatment are we beginning to understand the need for whole-body healing from both the east and west. I hope that one day we will have a unified and complete medical system that encompasses all systems of the world. Wouldn't that be something?

Personally, I'd like to see Qigong prescribed by doctors here in the west, much like they do in the hospitals in China. It's a great medicine.

Well, that's my goal anyway.

I'd like to have a school where anyone can just drop in off the street and have access to Qigong, meditation, yoga, health and nutrition education, cooking skills, life management, physical fitness, creative arts, music therapy and ways to learn how to express emotions, all under one roof!

Knowing that you are reading this book I am one step closer to my goal, so thank you again!

Now that we have a more informed idea of what we are physically made of, I hope you can agree that it's worth protecting and looking after our bodies a little more.

With a good diet and some daily Qigong, there's no reason why we can't all lead a happy and healthy life.

Now, let's move forward and put all this knowledge into practise.

Are you ready?

Student Notes

Chapter Six

How to Grow Your Qi!

The Three Phases of Developing Energy

Introduction

There are three main levels, or processes to the Qigong I share with students. Firstly, we practise to nourish and heal the physical body, then to nurture the mind and finally, to develop the spiritual self.

Many healing practices concentrate on using the mind to heal the body first, but I do not believe this to be as effective as starting with the physical body. The modern age is a busy and tense place for many people and physical relaxation seems to be the main priority for modern health.

It is also relatively easy to relax the mind by just taking time out and having some peace and quiet or meditation practise. This can be really tough if your hip is screaming at you or your back is cramping with pain. The patience needed to endure the discomfort while the body heals is beyond the acceptance of many beginners.

During my years of treating patients with Acupuncture, Tui Na and Qigong, every one of them has had some kind of pain that is causing them a degree of emotional stress, so that's where we will begin.

If we can remove the noise of the pain and injury, the mind will relax much easier and you will achieve a deeper state of relaxation.

Once the body and mind have the space to relax, you become more self-aware of your health and well-being then you will naturally develop a good foundation for future self-development and the practice of Qigong.

In our journey so far, you have learnt about the energy system and how it can be affected by illness and emotions. The practice of 'Finding Your Centre' in chapter four will help bring your body and mind into the present moment so you can begin building your awareness and be mindful of your health. We have also looked at how amazing our physical body is, so you can understand how important it is to look after it for better health.

So, now that you have all this wonderful information, I hope it has given you an insight into how amazing you really are, but more importantly how you can improve your own personal health with simple daily adjustments. Those changes begin right now with the three phases of our Qigong.

The Three Phases

The system that I share is divided into three phases. I call them phases because each leads into the next, much like the natural course of the seasons and cycles of life. Without each phase, the other phases will not be able to achieve their goal and potential. These phases are:

Preparation

Practise

Protection

Our initial preparation techniques help to gently move the joints and muscles, increase blood flow and release tensions in the body frame so we can get the very best from our Qigong session.

Phase one helps to shift and release the daily blockages we collect throughout life. As we age, the joints and junctions become increasingly stiff through lack of movement. Even a daily routine of the preparation methods has great benefits for all of us.

I must state now that the preparation phase is very important and is in no way meant to be skipped before practise if you want to really get the best benefits from your Qigong. Think of it as washing your car before applying the polish. Yes, you can go straight ahead and polish the car, but you will also be polishing the dirt and grime too! So, give yourself a nice hose down and rinse with the warm-up phase and really let the results shine through.

Before you can cultivate and grow your Qi you must prepare the body and mind, much like you would when cultivating the earth to grow crops. The better the soil, the better the crops.

When it comes to cultivating and growing Qi, the state of your mind and body are very important. The practise of Qigong amplifies the energy system so if you are tense, ill or experiencing any emotional stress then there's a good chance you could make things worse if you don't take a little time to prepare yourself first.

Once you become more adept at the practices you will have a better idea of how to prepare yourself when your health is in a less than satisfactory state of vigour, but for now go slow, and go steady. The warm-up section in this book contains just eight simple movements to release and connect the seven aspects of the body: the ankles, knees, hips, waist, shoulders, neck and arms. These help to move blood, release joints, and activate the muscle systems. As previously mentioned, just by itself and as a standalone practice, the warm-up routine has all the benefits of any other exercise system, and much, much more!

The Baduanjin

The second phase is the practise of the 'Eight Movements'. These movements are commonly known as the 'Eight Brocades' or Baduanjin pronounced (Ba Dwan Jin).

Baduanjin is one of the oldest known forms of Qigong and highly noted for its empowering effect on general health maintenance. It was also revised in the 1950s by some of China's athletic and health specialists so that they could devise a simple routine that could be practised by the majority of people to maintain health.

At the time, Baduanjin was promoted throughout schools, institutions and businesses. It is common in China for employees to practise Qigong before starting work so that they may deliver the best working day possible and feel on top form.

There are numerous versions of the Baduanjin so don't be confused if you see methods that differ from the ones I will share with you in this book. It's not necessarily what the movement looks like that has the health benefit, but rather, more about what is happening inside the body when the movements are performed.

The first set of Baduanjin I was taught originated from the Shaolin temple. It is very physical and orientated towards martial training. It was taught to me by my Taijiquan teacher at the time so that I could help my clinic patients with their recovery outside of the clinic. I will always be thankful for this as it started a whole new journey for me, personally and professionally.

Throughout my Qigong journey, I have experienced many other Qigong forms from other teachers and still find the Baduanjin to be the most effective and simple to learn. It literally does exactly what we require for better health:

Exercises the whole body and mind

Strengthens the bones and muscles

Calms emotions and releases trauma

I have since learned other systems of Baduanjin and continue to study and discuss variations with those that have studied it in depth. Each variation has a certain characteristic of its own, but essentially, they all stimulate the same aspects of the body and activate very similar energy paths. The techniques within this book are very simple to practise. This is what I teach to all new students, young and old.

I have met with people of all ages, different ranges of mobility, and varied medical conditions. For some of the movements, I have three different levels of practice to offer so that each student can progress as their body begins to strengthen and improve. This has allowed me to cater for the wide variety of people that I have had the pleasure to train with so far.

When we practise Qigong, we will usually have a specific aim in mind with every activity or external movement so there are certain checkpoints to adhere to, in order to get the best from each posture.

Each of the eight movements in the Baduanjin relates to a specific organ system, elemental energy, or its related vessel or fascia path. Each organ system also correlates to a specific emotion, sound, smell, taste, body tissue, colour and element of nature via the theory of the five elements in medicine.

I will include a short section on each of the movement pages that will explain the individual aspects in more detail so that you can begin to develop the idea and theory of TCM along with the five elements.

The third and final phase of practise is called 'sealing and closing' which help to keep our energy system protected. When we practise Qigong we are activating our whole essence of being, not just the physical parts. We are developing a connection or reconnection between our body and mind.

This practice helps to open the energy pathways so that the body and mind can heal and balance themselves. When we have finished with our healing work we need to centre our Qi and return our newly-restored energy back to our centre, the 'dantian' or 'energy well'.

This process helps to store our energy. It's like stoking up the fire of a wood burner, then closing the door so that the heat can be slowly dissipated, rather than leaving the door open for it to be wasted and the fire burn out quicker.

When we store our cultivated Qi, we allow it to glow gently and burn softly, maintaining our health and equilibrium within. Without this process of sealing in the good energy it can easily escape and be wasted. Or even worse, if our energies are low enough, as they are at times of ill health, we can leave ourselves open to damage from external sources such as other people, environmental factors or infectious diseases.

Even if you only do a very short session of Qigong - especially as a beginner - it pays to seal, close, and protect your health at every session. It's good to be centred!

Setting Your Mind

Before we get moving forward with the physical movement of Qigong, let's have a quick recap to develop the right mindset of what you are going to achieve. I have also included some practise advice to help you with your training.

Author's Tip

1. If you want to lead a happy and healthy life, balance is the key component. Leading a life full of physical strain and overdoing things will eventually take its toll on your health.

Make sure you include some 'me time' to nourish your body and mind. Taking time out will have great benefits for your personal health.

2. If you are feeling emotional, making time for physical activities will help release tension and stress, even a daily walk can make a huge difference.

Remember this: 'move it or lose it!'.

3. Be your own dynamo! Pedal too quickly and you might blow a bulb. Pedal too slowly and you won't have enough light to light the journey. Take it steady.

4. Spend time with your breath in the fresh air. Sit quietly and just breathe for ten minutes every day to help ignite the energy within.

5. Have a lifestyle clear-out, reduce the things in your life that affect your happiness. Learn to say 'no'.

6. Improve your foods. Remember the quality of food you eat has a direct effect on the energy you will feel. Without the right building blocks, it's easy to feel tired and achy.

7. Cherish your body. You are amazing and so are your bones, muscles, organs, fascia, tendons, ligaments, etc. This is the gift you have been given by your parents, care for it and enjoy it as much as possible.

8. Be the best you can be. Listen, learn and educate yourself in ways to improve your life experience. There are endless options available if you just keep looking.

9. Invest in your health! It will be the best thing you ever do. Just ten minutes every day can have a profound effect on pain and suffering.

10. Be the champion of your own life doing the things that make you feel connected and whole. Surround yourself with like-minded people, they will help you find your way.

Now that we have set our minds and connected to our breath, let's move forward with the active components of our Qigong practice.

Practice Advice

In order to get the very best from your practice there are a few things to keep in mind before you start. These are general advice tips that have been noted in every piece of Qigong literature I have read, and also passed down by every teacher to students. They are not set in stone, but they will help make your experience of Qigong more enjoyable.

Suitable Clothing

It is advisable to wear natural fibre materials when practising Qigong. Synthetic or tight clothing not only creates false heat but also helps contain static energy and heat as the body tries to release energy during practise.

You should always be a comfortable temperature so having a light jumper or cardigan that can be easily removed or added during training is a good idea.

Suitable Footwear

Footwear should be simple, flat and comfortable. During practise we are aiming to improve spinal health. Some modern forms of footwear can affect our true central awareness and even cause many postural problems.

Never practise on a full stomach!

You should observe the rule 'Half Full, Half Empty'. The recommended time for practise is one hour to 90 minutes following a heavy or large meal.

Practising with a full stomach will interrupt the digestive systems and could cause problems. Practising while hungry will become a distraction and the full benefits or energy work cannot be achieved.

Hydration

The practice of Qigong requires the use of both the body and mind. You will excite body parts you may not have used for a while so the body can easily become dehydrated. Have a warm drink handy to stay focused and fresh.

Cautionary Notes

If you experience any pain or discomfort, strong emotions, headaches, dizziness or anything that you are unsure about, close down your practise and stop training. Have a warm drink and maybe a light snack and rest.

Remember Qigong should be an enjoyable experience and only you know how you are feeling at any given moment so take it easy and go with your instincts.

You can always return to your training later, or on another day. There's no rush with Qigong.

Chapter Seven

Preparing the Vessels

Building the Foundations

Introduction

Now that we have set our minds it's time to get our energy moving. This section of the book is where we get started building a great daily routine of health and well-being.

Preparing the body helps you get the best from your practice and reconnect the body parts that often get disconnected by lack of use through modern duties.

The body consists of numerous parts that all work together to maintain our optimum health and functions, but this can easily be disturbed by many of the activities modern life has created.

If we go back to simpler times, way before televisions, computers and mobile technology, our bodies were in much better use daily. If you had to travel, you walked, for food, you farmed, when you were hungry, you cooked and when you were tired, you rested. All these duties kept us mobile and active, mentally and physically.

This is in total contrast to today's lifestyles where many jobs are sedentary. Our use of cars to travel keeps us seated, when we watch television we are seated. And now, with mobile devices, although we are not always seated when we use them, we are however constantly leaning forward and bending the tops of our spines and necks to see the information on our phones, tablets and laptops. Unfortunately, we all love these devices so much that most of us are not prepared to see the destruction they are causing our bodies, especially because the damage is so gradual.

This gives even more value to the practice of Qigong as it helps to counteract these modern troubles by reminding you to stand upright, move your whole body, rotate your joints, excite the muscles and most of all, stimulate your mind!

So, with each of the following movements we gradually reconnect the body. Starting with the ankles through the legs and hips. Onward through the waist, torso and spine. From the arms to the fingers and upwards through the neck, finally reaching our powerhouse, our brain.

This amazing system helps to remind us that we are, in all our glory, designed to stand and walk tall on two legs, not crouch and bend like monkeys.

How to use this book

Each of the following illustrations provides an informative guide to the correct practise of the movement in this book. Where needed, actions and advice have been included to complement the drawings. Please use the information on this page to develop an understanding of the illustrations throughout this book and what they mean.

Shaded pathways on the body of the illustrations provide a guide to areas where changes or tension in the tissues can be felt.

Do not worry if you do not feel this, everyone is different and through regular practise you will feel the connections.

All movements should be performed in a relaxed and controlled manner. The idea is to feel any tension and then release it gently.

The arrows signify a direction of movement or awareness.

E.g. In this illustration the body sinks downwards and there is a sensation of moving the knees apart in opposite directions.

There is a slight rotation of the waist as the arm moves outward.

Remember to relax and enjoy each posture as you move through the pages of this section.

Position the feet so that they are pointing forward and parallel. Due to the difference in body types, the feet can move slightly outward. Above all else, there should be no strain on the knee joints.

1. Swinging the Arms

Swinging the arms gently increases blood and Qi circulation. It helps to relax the shoulders and neck by gently promoting blood flow into the area with each swing.

The natural pendulum-like movement has an additional relaxing effect on the mind. Remember to keep the knees soft so that you can begin connecting to the earth.

Practise

1. Stand the feet at shoulder width apart. Soften the knees and relax into the feet.

2. Gently swing your arms back and forth, forward and back in a relaxed motion.

3. Repeat 150-300 times or set a timer for 3-5 minutes.

2. Step Forward, Sink Back

This movement helps to relax the hips and lower back while stimulating the front and back fascia pathways of our energy vessels: stomach and bladder, our earth and water. It also assists in promoting the circulation of blood to nourish the whole body.

Practise

1. Stand the feet shoulder width apart.

2. Turn the right foot slightly outward and take a step forward with the left foot.

3. Gently push off the right foot lifting the heel off the ground to engage the sole of the foot, the calf muscle and the back of the leg.

4. Return the right foot to the ground and shift the weight of the body onto the rear leg. Slowly lift up the left toes.

5. Sink the body weight returning the left foot to the ground. Begin pushing forward with the right leg. Repeat 10-20 times.

6. Step back into shoulder width stance and rest. Turn the left foot outward 45 degrees. Take a small step forward with the right foot and repeat as per the left side.

Author's Tip

Try to be aware of the body tissues that engage throughout all the movements in this book. We are trying to stimulate the energy vessels and promote relaxation. When the tissue pathways are activating by each movement you may feel the changes in the body.

This feeling can be a light tightness or restriction like a mild stretch. When I teach Qigong to students I do not use the word stretch as I feel it conveys thoughts of pulling two ends away from each other like an elastic band.

What we are trying to achieve is an 'opening' of the tissues by having a relaxed and gentle intent or being mindful of our actions as we perform the physical movements.

This develops our mind-body connections and gives our practise the holistic results that improve our health.

3. Rotating the Ankle

Movement three in our preparation starts to build our root for the following training methods. While one side is strong and stable, the other is soft and agile. The outward rotation helps to release the hips and lower back while softening the knee and ankle.

Practise

1. From a shoulder width stance shift the weight over onto the right leg and take a small step backwards with the left foot resting on the ball of the foot.

2. Gently rotate the ankle outward keeping the ball of the foot on the floor. Repeat 10-20 times.

3. Step back into shoulder width stance and shift the weight over onto the left leg. Take a step back with the right foot. Rotate the ankle outwards 10-20 times.

Author's Tip

Try to relax the whole leg from the hip. You should have a sense of gently massaging the foot into the earth. Make sure you travel in a circular motion around the tips of the toes and ball of the foot.

Not only does this simple movement release the ankle through its motion but it also relaxes the hip joint and knee joint. In terms of TCM, it also serves to massage the 'bubbling well' (Kidney 1) point on the sole of the foot which has many health benefits for the body in general.

4. Turning the Waist

The waist is very important as it is the pathway between the upper and lower parts of the body. It houses the lower digestive system so any form of movement, exercise or relaxation in this area will help stimulate both the large and small intestines and help the body absorb energy and eliminate waste.

The lower Jiao (the area below the navel) houses the bladder. To an extent, movement of this area also engages the outer abdominal muscles that run from our hips to our ribs and the lower lumbar groups. This gently massages the kidneys, both of which help to eliminate fluid waste and oxidant substances that affect the smooth operation of the whole body.

This simple but effective movement is paramount in modern times with the increase of sedentary occupations, media entertainment and long-distance driving. Turning the waist can help restore and replenish stagnant energy developed by lack of motion in the middle-body system.

If you ever find yourself waiting for the kettle to boil, the toast to pop up in the toaster or if you have a spare minute in between daily duties, just take a step out to the side, relax into the feet and make a few gentle turns of the waist in each direction. Doing this can give you a short energy boost so you won't feel as if you need another expresso or chocolate biscuit to get by!

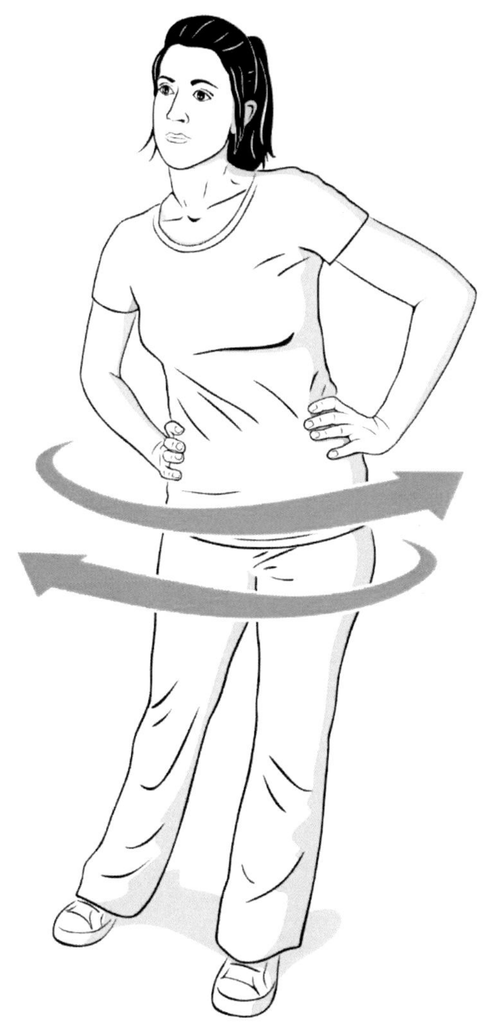

Practise

1. Stand in a shoulder width stance. Soften the knees and relax the body weight into the feet.

2. Rest the backs of the hands in the small of the back or on the sides of the hips.

3. Gently circle the waist clockwise 10-20 times. Return to centre.

4. Gently circle the waist anti-clockwise 10-20 times. Return to centre.

Author's Tip

Using the following illustration, *(Fig 7.1)* start in the centre and move your hips to the left.

Continue to move the centre of the body in a circle trying to pass through the eight points.

You could also imagine you have a big hoop around your waist. Try to move the body around the surface of the hoop as you circle the waist.

Start slowly allowing the hips and lower back to relax in a smooth rotational movement.

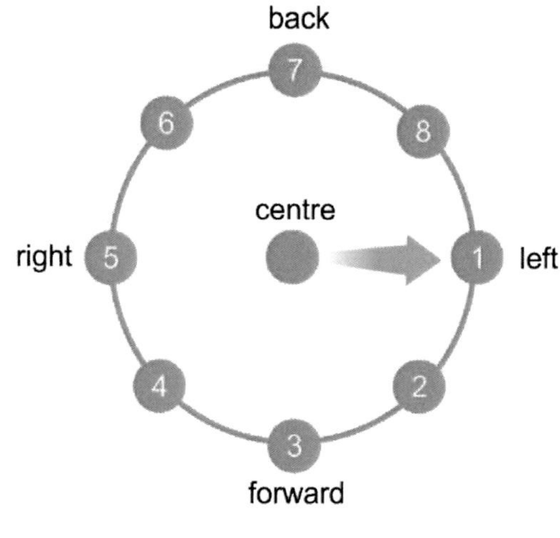

(Fig 7.1)

Rotating the waist movement

As you progress through your practice, the rotations become softer and more tension is released which is great for any painful ankle symptoms, knees, hips, spine or neck.

Turning the waist is a simple exercise that can be practised at any time to help maintain mobility in the hips and lower back.

Student Notes

5. Swimming with the Spine

Each of the following movements helps to relax the hips, lower back and spine. The arm rotations create a mild rotation of the spine to reduce pressure on the nerves.

Practise

1. Gently circle the arms and hands forward past the ear in a 'front crawl' swimming-style movement 10-20 times.

2. Relax the waist so that the spine naturally rotates. Try to keep the elbows and shoulders as relaxed as you can.

3. Slowly come to a stop.

4. Leading with the elbows, gently fold the arms backward, circling down and around.

5. Repeat 10–20 times. Be aware that the elbow and shoulder must remain relaxed.

Finish forward movements 10 times.

Author's Tip

Relax the hips and legs into the feet so the spine can rotate naturally and freely.

6. Pulling down the Heavens

Our next movement is one of the most common postures across many Qigong systems. It opens the whole body and gently creates a grounding or rooting sensation as the body softens through the framework into the feet.

This is also a posture that I use a lot when closing my training session. It has a wonderful calming effect on the body and mind.

You can also practise this movement as a stand-alone posture to really get the energy softly moving and relax the physical body.

Practise

1. Stand in a shoulder width stance.

2. Place the hands at the sides of the body. Palms facing the legs.

3. Imagine you have two balloons under each hand resting on the side of the thigh muscles.

4. Gently allow the balloons to float up at the sides, palms facing down on top of the balloons.

5. When the balloons reach shoulder height, rotate the palms to face upward.

6. Continue raising the hands in an upward arching movement.

7. As the hands reach up above the head, gently fold the palms into the centre.

8. Bring the hands downward in front of the body relaxing the

shoulders, elbows, wrists and then the palms.

9. Gently press at the end of the movement as if pushing clouds away.

10. Return the hands to the sides.

11. Repeat 10-20 times.

12. Return to centre.

Author's Tip

Pulling down the Heavens is a great way to begin regulating and conditioning the breath.

Breathe in as you raise the hands upward and then breathe out as you lower the arms. Try to perform the movement in time with your personal breathing pattern.

If at first it seems too hard to think about the breathing as well, just concentrate on making the movement soft and fluid and breathe naturally.

Final Preparation

Once you have completed the warm-up section, take a minute or so to gather the breath and perform the following methods.

These simple methods aim to clear and calm the energy system ready for your daily routine of Qigong.

Return to Centre

Stand in a shoulder width stance.

Soften the knees.

Sink the body weight into the feet.

Place the hands-on top of each other just below the navel.

Relax your breathing for 10 breaths.

Closing

Pull down the Heavens 5 times.

Return to centre for 10 breaths.

Warm the Kidneys

Warm the palms and massage the lower back until warm. If the palms do not warm immediately, clap the hands a few times to get the blood moving into the palms.

NB. Never place cold palms on the lower back, the kidneys do not like the cold!

Shaking

Rest the backs of the hands on the small of the back or sides of the hips.

Gently begin to bounce up and down on the feet allowing the body to gently shake. Repeat 30 times.

Conclusion

Now that you have completed the basic warm-up and preparation system, spend some time getting to know the movements and how your body feels when you are practising.

The preparation practice is a great time to release any tensions and also activate any tired or stiff muscles. The warm-up system in itself is a very simple method for improving health, so practise it whenever you can.

I regularly teach and prescribe this to patients for many weeks to prepare their bodies for further treatment. The simple stuff is sometimes always the best.

Practise, Practise, Practise!

This Chinese text is a personal motto I like to keep in mind, it means perseverance.

The general translation of this Chinese text means to 'not concern yourself with being a master of one thing but be more mindful of your daily practice'.

This motto always keeps my training simple. I do not waste my energy on thinking about being a master of Qigong, this is not my goal. I know if I regularly practise, I will be moving closer towards better health and happiness.

Life changes on a daily basis and what you want for yourself right now might not be what you desire later on. I remember a student once asked me 'can you make me a master?' to which I replied, 'what would you like to be a master of?'. The conversation ended.

I'm not entirely sure you can be a master of Qigong. To me this is not important. There are far more important things to master first.

Why not become a master of your digestion or lifestyle? A master of your job, a master of compassion, a master of being a parent, a master of teaching, a master of happiness or indeed anything at which you'd like to excel. This is what makes our life journey more enjoyable.

Be your own master and let Qigong be the vehicle to get you there, in style!

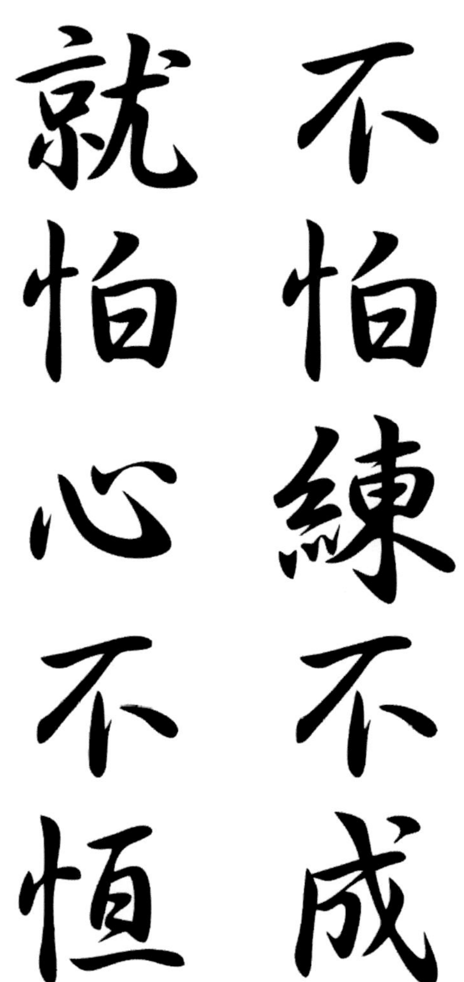

'Perseverance'

Student Notes

Each and every day is an opportunity to make health better, no matter how little.

A five-minute walk, swapping a packet of crisps for some fruit, soaking in the bath, unplugging from the digital world, visiting a friend or closing your eyes to just breathe.

These are all very practical methods that gradually build into a better, brighter life.

Chapter Eight

The 'Eight Movements'

Activating the Body's Own Medicine

Baduanjin Introduction

The next section is all about the practice of our eight main movements, the Baduanjin.

As previously mentioned in the introduction to the warm-up and preparation, we are 'connecting' the body parts together with each movement. Now that we have stimulated the whole body we can move forward to our main practise of the Baduanjin, which goes even further to reconnect the body and mind.

Not only do the movements work to exercise the major muscle groups: the legs, arms, shoulders, abdomen, back and chest areas, it also works on the deeper muscles and tendons that are responsible for maintaining our structure and integrity.

The smaller muscles and tendons in our body are the ones that keep us mobile, flexible and feeling youthful. They also help to keep the joints and bones together and strong, so we reduce the chances of injuries and pain.

Many modern illnesses and symptoms present themselves in the joints and spine so maintaining a healthy and youthful structure could be the key to a long and enjoyable life.

There is a saying in Chinese Martial Arts: 'long tendons, long life' and this is exactly what they mean.

Each posture or movement stimulates, opens, (stretches) and excites a specific area or part of the body. Through the practise of the Baduanjin, all aspects and tissue structures are exercised and conditioned to provide a complete and nourishing physical workout.

This gentle workout removes the tensions in the structure and immediately improves blood circulation to reach all parts of the body and mind. Less tension means less stress. Less stress means calmer emotions.

What else could we possibly need?

Take your time and enjoy every section of the eight movements. As you move through them, let all the tensions just flow out of your body and mind. Remember to smile and breathe naturally.

Good Luck!

What are the Vessels?

I thought I would include a further discussion on the energy vessels so you can begin to form an idea of how they fit into our Qigong practice.

Most of you who are familiar with energy work may know of 'meridians' or perhaps you are aware of a network of pathways that Qi is thought to move around the body.

As previously mentioned, each organ has a related pairing of vessels that spans across the body, through the muscles and joints to complete an endless circuit of power or life force.

At specific points on these vessels, the resistance of energy changes or 'pools'. These 'energy pools' are where the vessels are most affected by changes and can be stimulated to adjust the activity in the related pathway.

Stimulation of these points is commonly made using acupuncture needles or by applying pressure by hand, as in the practice of acu-pressure and massage. The points can also be affected by applications of heat, cold, herbs and transdermal therapies. Qigong practice also stimulates the points through specific movements.

Various points can also be used to release tensions in the muscle and tissue systems that are not necessarily related to the area being stimulated.

Physical manipulation of these energy pools can have a profound effect on the physical and emotional mind. Once my students have grasped their practice of Qigong, I begin to introduce them to Tui Na and the applications of self-applied massage methods. This provides great benefits to health and the convenience of being able to continually treat your own ailments throughout the day until the condition or symptoms have subsided is a real advantage.

Being able to help yourself in hours of discomfort is a great tool to have. The massage techniques will also help your friends, families and children in times of need. The results can be very therapeutic to a distressed child or a welcome relief to a partner after a long day at work.

Let's face it, everyone loves a neck and shoulder massage at the end of the day!

I plan to write about this system in another volume so once you have your daily Qigong routine in hand, you can progress forward to learn how to treat yourself with Qigong Massage.

As you can see by the illustration, the pathways span the body in many ways. If you look at the bladder vessel (marked in blue) you understand that problems in this pathway may cause pain and discomfort in the spine. You could also experience neck pain or headaches as the bladder vessel travels upward over the head to the bridge of the nose.

Looking at the gall bladder vessel (marked in green) at its upper end, it encompasses a large area of the head. Its main symptoms can be headaches, neck pain and tension across the shoulders. It also spans to the eye and ear which could present as problems with hearing, eye irritations, migraines or stiffness in the jaw, much like the small intestine vessel.

The gall bladder in TCM commonly relates to the emotions and it's not uncommon to feel drained, forgetful or have problems making life decisions if the gall bladder vessel is not clear and functioning efficiently. These are just a few of the possible ailments shown in this illustration.

As mentioned previously in chapter two, the complete vessel system has twelve main vessels and six 'extraordinary' vessels that reach from head to toe intertwining and branching out to reach all parts of the body giving access to many possibilities for treatment.

I have included some of these pathways in the following illustrations to give you a simple idea how each movement affects its related vessel.

Hopefully this brief introduction will plant a seed of interest in you and enliven your spirit for more knowledge of TCM and holistic practice.

Know Your Flow

The 'Eight Movements' in this book follow the natural flow of the daily energy circuit. Every time you practise you are gently nudging your energy in the right direction. This helps to remove and reduce blockages that can cause pain and illness.

Maintaining the correct flow of Qi in the vessels means that there is less chance for the organs to lose their harmonious balance as they are able to support each other with the right amount of power.

This also means that there are fewer fluctuations in the system so we feel more balanced in our minds and bodies.

The initial stage for any new student is to remember the correct order of practise, so please take some time to learn each phase of the system and devise a memory cue that will help you remember.

1. 'Lifting the Sky' - To Regulate the Triple Heater

I like to think of the first movement as the one that 'gets the motor running'. It uses the whole body to perform the movement and creates an overall opening of the three major core sections or Jiao.

'Lifting the Sky' provides a release of the internal organs and tissue systems to gently massage the three cavities and their respective organs. This will improve the functions of the whole body, increase nutritional uptake and help to promote efficient elimination of waste.

The posture works to stimulate what is known as the Sanjiao or Triple Heater. The upward expanding motion creates a concertina effect internally, gently releasing the central core of the body by squeezing and releasing the organ systems. I often refer to it as the action of bellows being used.

The upper burner, or Jiao, is the region above the sternum, the neck and chest area. It contains the heart and lungs which help to move blood and oxygen around the body.

The middle Jiao contains the stomach, spleen and liver which are responsible for the process of accepting food and breaking it down for digestion, but also separating the pure fluids from the waste.

The lower Jiao contains the bladder, large and small intestines which deal with elimination of waste from the body.

Although the kidneys span both the middle and lower burners they are considered a lower burner organ as they deal with elimination.

'Lifting the Sky' is beneficial for all aspects of the body but most importantly for the internal working of the organs. It's a great movement in preparation for any energy work and can be used as a simple stand-alone practice in its own right.

If you keep in mind that you are supporting the sky with this movement it will allow you to remain soft and pliable throughout. Supporting has a com-passionate and trustworthy quality.

As you reach the hands above the head, gently allow all the body tissues to open from the feet right up to the hands. Then release any tension in the tissues and return to the start position.

Author's Tip

Caution: Raising the hands above the head may increase blood pressure so be careful if you suffer with hypertension. Do not force the movement but allow it to happen naturally.

Practise

1. Stand in shoulder width stance.

2. Lift both hands, palms facing upward, up to chest height.

3. Rotate the hands and forearms as they pass the face and push towards the sky.

4. Rotate wrists so that the palms face downward and lower the hands gently in front of the body.

5. When the arms have reached the full extent, circle the hands and begin to gather the palms upward ready to repeat movement.

6. Repeat 8 times.

2. 'Archer Draws His Bow' - To Benefit the Lungs

Our journey of the energy circuit always begins with the lungs. The lung organs sit at the top of the table when it comes to Qi. With every breath we take, air energy is propelled into our lungs, providing our bodies with the oxygen we need for all the functions that keep us alive every day.

The lungs are often thought of as the delicate organs, like the leaves on the tips of the tree's branches, taking in light, warmth and water. They also soak up the unhealthy gases in the atmosphere and literally recycle the air, sending out new and usable air for us to breathe.

The lungs help to expel excess water and heat from the body every time we breathe out. As the lungs are delicate they can be easily damaged by heat, damp and dryness. Living or working in dry environments dehydrates the lungs causing dry coughs, irritation, water retention and of course, dehydration. Damp environments can cause phlegm to accumulate in the lungs, leaving us hoarse or congested.

The lungs are closely related to our skin which is sometimes considered to be the 'third lung'. The skin literally 'breathes' to release fluids and heat just like the lung. It is also a physical protective layer to the outside world, much like the lungs, our first line of defence against external germs and bacteria.

It is common to see people with weak lung energy suffer with asthma, dry skin conditions, fluid retention in the skin (oedema) or even emotional problems like depression and sadness because there is a lack of vital energy from efficient breathing, or the respiratory muscles have become weak.

If the functionality of the lungs becomes weak, there is an immediate loss of oxygen and the mind may feel anxious for the body as a whole. Its only remedy is to reduce or cease movement so that it can make the best use of the resources it has at that particular time.

Physical exercise to increase the functionality of the lungs and ultimately increase oxygen levels can be a very simple remedy for many low mood disorders.

Practise

1. Stand out to the side in a wider than shoulder width stance. Cross the hands in front of your chest with right hand in front, palms facing chest. Sink the weight into the feet and lower the body slightly.

2. Loosely clench the left hand as if grasping the string of a bow. At the same time the right hand forms a pointing shape with the thumb out, and the index finger straight upward.

3. Raise up the left elbow and pull back as if drawing a bow. Simultaneously move the right arm out to the right until it is fully extended but not locked.

4. Now gather the right hand in an arc at shoulder height and return it to the chest. Relax the left hand back towards the body sinking the elbow to rest in front of the chest. You are now back at the beginning. The left hand should be in front of the right.

5. Grasp the bow with the right hand and turn the left hand into a pointed hand ... continue.

6. Repeat 4 times each side.

Author's Tip

There are many things you can do every day to improve the functionality of the lungs in conjunction with your daily Qigong practice. Good respiratory function means that our Qi can work its magic.

Here are just a few suggested activities:

1. Sitting upright. If you have a job that keeps you seated at a desk all day, take action regularly. The sitting position can often reduce the capacity of the chest cavity as you bend over your desk each day. This reduces your ability to take deep and useful breaths, breathing becomes shallow and eventually the lungs may weaken.

Try to sit upright and stop every now and then to remind yourself to take deep and meaningful breaths. This will also help maintain your posture and possibly reduce any problems in the future.

2. Get fresh air. This is common sense really. The better the air quality, the better use it will be when it enters the body. Try to get regular fresh air daily. A short walk is best or try to open a window if you are doing your Qigong inside.

3. Reduce external heat. External heat such as that produced by household heating systems, artificial heating or heating such as you find in a bakery. All contribute to dryness and fluid imbalances.

If you cannot change the environment, you can use plants, pots of water or air misters to keep the air humid. You can also drink more water or fluid-filled foods such as melon, cucumber and fruits which help to maintain hydration.

4. Let go of loss. The lungs are commonly affected by loss. Experiencing loss can feel like a weight has been added to the lungs creating a restriction and stagnation that prevents us from moving forward in life.

That weight is often felt in the shoulders as both the lungs and large intestine vessels run through the chest and shoulders.

We will all experience grief and loss during our lives. For many of us, this will affect our lungs and thus maintaining our deep breathing is paramount to reducing painful or energy-draining illnesses.

Student Notes

3. 'Plucking the Stars' - To Regulate the Stomach and Spleen

Our third posture relates to the earth phase of the five elements: the stomach and spleen. This organ pairing is responsible for our intake of food nutrition. The stomach receives the food we eat and begins the process of converting this to energy. The spleen separates the pure from the turbid and begins the conversion of food and fluids into blood and Qi.

The quality of our blood and Qi is a direct result of the food we provide the body. Poor diet inevitably means poor health, or at least a reduced quality of energy. The spleen is also responsible for transporting and transforming fluids in the body.

The stomach and spleen, our earth organs, like a balanced environment to feel happy. The stomach dislikes excessive damp foods like fats and sugars and the spleen dislikes excessive amounts of cold, raw foods.

One of the easiest ways to injure the spleen and cause digestive issues is by consuming too many ice-cold drinks or maintaining a diet of cold energy foods that are raw and uncooked. The most immediate effect of this is fatigue and loose bowel movements.

Our earth organs, when unbalanced, can manifest as worry and to an extent, mild feelings of anxiety. When this organ system is out of balance, we can overthink our thoughts, feel stuck, lose our appetite or suffer with muscle pains and fatigue.

Some conditions that arise from an imbalance in the earth organs are digestive complaints like IBS, worrying about trivial things and events, looking backwards to the past and yearning.

It can also affect our memory and our ability to concentrate. Thinking can become muzzy and dull, sometimes accompanied by a feeling of heaviness in the head and body. Everything becomes oppressive and slow, like being stuck in the mud.

'Plucking the Stars' is a great move for general energy boosting. If you feel fatigued or lethargic, then this practice will help revive a tired body and mind.

3. At the full extent, roll the hand facing upwards over so that the palm is facing downward. Turn the right hand below so that the palm is facing up.

4. Bring the hands back to the starting chest position. The hands will be in the inverse position to when you started, left palm facing down, right palm facing up.

5. Repeat 4 times each side.

Practise

1. Place the hands in front of the chest at a level with the lower ribs. Left palm is facing up. Right palm is facing down.

2. Raise the left hand upward rotating the hand so that the palm is facing upward as it passes the face and push to the sky. Simultaneously push downward with the right hand.

4. 'Turning the Head' - To Eliminate Harmful Feelings

Our fourth posture moves into the fire element and stimulates the small intestine vessel which is responsible for deriving the last of the goodness from the food we eat as it passes through the first section of the bowels for elimination as waste.

Along with the spleen, the small intestine is affected by worry which can cause it to stagnate in energy. This can result in abdominal pains, flatulence, constipation, diarrhoea and emotional vagueness.

Hot foods such as spices can injure this organ and too much heat can rise to agitate the emotions of frustration and anger. As the small intestine focuses on collecting the last of the pure essence from foods, it also has an effect on our energy levels, so feelings of tiredness and fatigue are common when this organ is out of balance.

The vessel travels from the little finger upward on the outer aspect of the arm and navigates through the scapula, continuing upward to the side of the neck, across the cheek and to the ear notch.

Physical problems like a stiff neck with reduced ability to turn the head, pain of the jaw, restrictions in the shoulder blade and numbness or tingling in the hands can all be a result of restriction in the small intestine pathway.

It also helps to reduce weary and detrimental feelings that can be felt by the inability to turn the head. Many of you will have experienced driving a car with a stiff neck and not being able to see over your shoulder at a junction or interchange. This can fill you with feelings of fear and vulnerability, so this movement helps to restore a certain amount of confidence by increasing our range of movement.

Author's Tip

If you experience any dizziness or feel unbalanced when you turn the eyes, refrain from doing this part of the movement. In some cases, this can be a sign of a cervical problem that requires a professional assessment.

Practise

1. Stand shoulder width apart. Rest the backs of the hands in the small of the back to relax the shoulders.

2. Be mindful that the head is a ball on top of a pole. Allow it to rest naturally. Raise the crown and relax into the feet.

3. Using the tip of the nose as a point of reference, slowly turn the head horizontally to the right until you can feel a slight restriction in the neck tissues.

4. Gently turn the eyes to look behind.

5. Repeat 4 times each side.

Author's Extra Tip

Always be mindful that the head is a ball on top of a pole, gently resting and balancing its weight. If you remember to feel suspended from the crown, as in the 'Ten Checkpoints', it will help to relax the neck and shoulders.

As you can see from the illustration, the fascia train of the small intestine runs from the little finger to the neck and face.

Common problems along this line are: elbow pain; shoulder pain; stiff neck; jaw pain and problems associated with the ears. Restrictions in the vessel can also cause neck pain and recurring headaches.

5. 'Wagging the Head and Tail' - To Cool the Heart's Fire

Number five in our eight movements relates to the heart and fire. This movement helps to promote blood flow by lowering the body to activate the large muscles of the legs, hips and spine.

This slightly demanding movement requires an increase in blood flow to feed the muscles, therefore creating more activity in the heart to circulate blood. This lowering and activating movement also raises body heat that moves to the surface where it can be released through the skin pores.

The process helps to regulate body heat and maintain good health of the heart muscle which can become weak through lack of physical movement and reduced blood circulation.

This movement should be performed under full awareness and control. It is more important to concentrate on the lowering and stabilising of the legs throughout the posture rather than the depth of lowering the head.

Try to keep the head in line with the spine throughout the whole posture. Over time the hips will open and relax allowing the body to sink deeper. Be mindful to lower the top half of the body by hinging at the hips and not bending the spine.

If you have high or low blood pressure, start very slowly at a comfortable height. You can also use the hands to support the weight of the upper body to maintain control.

Maintaining a healthy heart is something we can all do by keeping ourselves moving. Regular gentle exercise is enough to keep us going for many years. Most heart-related problems I see in clinic are caused by lack of movement followed by poor diet choices and stress.

If you have persistent troubling emotions that stem from family and love, now is the time to sort things out before the physical heart suffers too!

Practise

1. Take a stance double shoulder width and turn the body at the waist to face right.

(Generally, the back foot points outwards 45 degrees and the front foot points forwards. Go with whatever feels natural without causing discomfort to the hips and knees.)

3. Turn the waist gently to the left in a controlled swing-like movement.

4. Gently raise up the body to face to the left. Pause.

5. Lower the body over the left leg while supporting the upper body.

6. Repeat 4 times each side.

Author's Tip

You can use the arms rested on the thighs to support the upper body while performing this movement.

2. Slowly lower the body over the leg, hinging at the hip.

6. 'Carrying the Moon' - To Strengthen the Kidneys and Waist

Our sixth posture is found in many Qigong systems in slightly different variations. 'Carrying the moon' relates to the kidneys so it's great for lower back pain and symptoms of fatigue, it really does wake the whole body and instils a calm sense of well-being.

In TCM the kidneys are closely related to our immune system and the way that fluids move around the body. The unwanted waste is sent to the lungs and expelled with respiration and the rest sent to the bladder to be eliminated in our urine.

As the kidneys are paired with the bladder, it is common to see weakness of the bladder and frequent urination when the kidneys' energies are diminished. Pain of the lower back that feels like a dull nagging ache, especially in the morning, is another sign and this posture can help relieve that annoying daily pain.

The bladder vessel runs from head to toe so 'carrying the moon' helps to relieve many symptoms along its pathway.

Common ailments that can be helped are calf and hamstring pain, restless legs and discomfort in the spinal column, even emotional pain and frontal headaches will benefit from this movement.

Practise

1. Stand in a central posture with feet around hip width apart.

2. Place hands together in front of the abdomen as if holding a balloon.

3. Carefully, while hinging at the hips, slowly lower the balloon to the floor until you feel a change in the tissue at the back of the legs. Relax the shoulder to lower the ball a little further.

4. When you have reached a comfortable flexion of the waist, begin to raise the arms straight and in an outward arch, maintaining a connection with the rear of the legs.

5. When the arms are level with the ears, begin to raise the head and body in line with the arms.

6. When you have reached an upward posture, open the hands to form a circle between the thumbs and index fingers as if carrying a ball.

7. Separate the hands to the sides, lowering them in an arch and straighten the body.

8. Repeat 8 times.

Author's Tip

For an extra nourishing treat to release the lower back and to stimulate the kidneys further, after each movement you can place the hands on the lower back and gently massage the area to warm the kidneys. This feels really comforting!

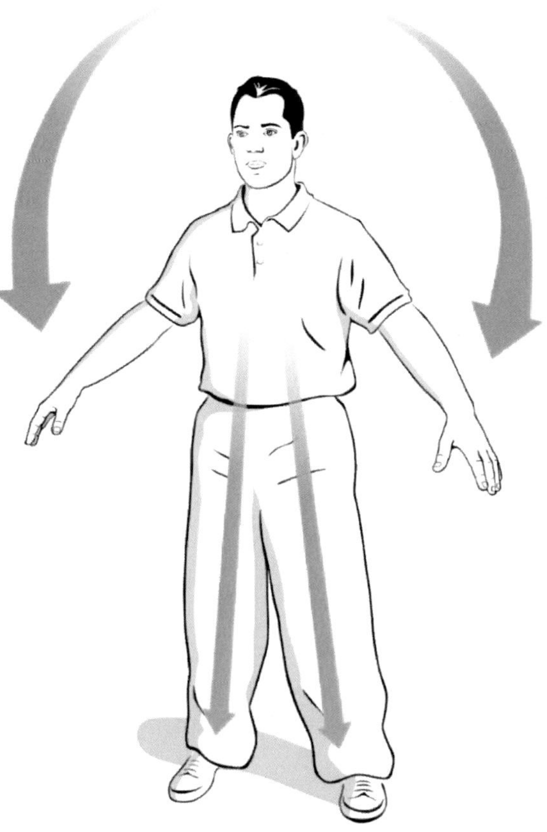

7. 'Thrusting the Fists' - To Benefit the Liver

Posture seven is a powerhouse for releasing tension and feelings of resentment, anger or frustration. The posture relates to our liver energy which helps us to grow throughout life - like the element of wood - as the tree grows from a seed into a majestic wonder of life.

This transformation helps us to grow as a person through life and maintains our sense of well-being and flow in our daily lives.

When the liver energy is affected we can feel quite differently, as if we are stuck in the mud, life is holding us back from our true nature or we can feel smothered and unable to progress with the life we want.

The liver is easily affected by unforeseen changes like the high winds that taunt the branches of a tree. It can also coil like a spring and explode into anger when pressed too hard by restrictions in life's journey.

Our relationships play a great role in the health of the liver. Past traumas, resentments and holding onto feelings can cause the emotions to swirl and stagnate if they are not released, or scatter, leaving us feeling lost and disconnected.

Blood is also closely related to the liver and common problems like stabbing pains in the abdomen, numbness in the limbs and tension in the muscles are all symptoms of an underperforming liver.

Practise

1. Take a stance slightly wider than shoulder width, lower the body.

2. Place the hand in loose fists at the sides of the chest under the armpits.

3. Push the right fist outward to the front level with the chest. At full extent, release the hand, palm faces downward.

4. Turn the palm to face upward and return hand into a loose fist and back to starting position.

5. Repeat on left side.

Author's Tip

Lowering the body helps to activate the large leg muscles which promote blood circulation to aid stagnation of energy.

The strengthening of the lower body also provides a feeling of being rooted and grounded to the earth so the emotions can be dissipated.

Try to relax into the hips making sure the knees do not extend over the toes.

When you extend the fist, slowly pull back the rear arm to stimulate the liver area.

Release and open the front hand as though dropping a stone into a pond.

Imagine gently grabbing the floor with the toes like the roots of a tree embedding themselves into the earth.

Extend the legs outward to increase the strength of the roots. Open the eyes slightly wider and gaze intently into the distance to stimulate the liver pathway which in TCM opens into the eyes.

8. 'Lifting the Heels' - To Stimulate the Spine and Posture

Our eighth and final posture is very simple. It aims to stimulate the spine and promote balance and posture as a whole-body movement.

Within each of the spaces of the spinal joints the nerves emerge to communicate with the rest of the body. Any restrictions or muscle tightness in this area can easily cause messages to become misplaced so a healthy and mobile spine is of utmost importance to overall body-mind functions. So, keep it moving and free!

Complete awareness of the entire body structure is needed to perform the movement.

Practise

1. Stand with feet hip width or closer together so you can maintain balance.

2. Raise the body upward onto the toes, stretching through the legs and spine to the crown as if being gently lifted by a piece of string. Breathe in as you lift.

3. At full extent, exhale while lowering the body gently onto the heels.

4. Repeat 8 times.

Conclusion

Now that you have experienced the eight movements of the Baduanjin, it is now yours to practise and enjoy throughout life. It can be hard to believe that such a simple system can have so much benefit, especially when it seems like just a simple exercise system, much like many others.

The difference here is that each movement has been specifically designed to have a deliberate effect. Generations of healers and students have created Qigong systems with the aim of improving health, reducing illness and preventing many diseases that cause pain and suffering.

In the beginning, it may feel a little strange as you are using the body in ways you may never have before. The Baduanjin works on parts of the body that you might not have used since you were a child!

When these connections become restored you will soon experience what it's like to be in good health and hopefully this will provide the incentive to discover even more about Qigong.

Here is a quick reference list to the full system of practice so you can see how simple it really is.

Preparation Warm-up

- Swing the arms
- Step forward both sides
- Turn the waist
- Swim arms forward and back
- Pull down the heavens
- Gather your centre

Eight Movements

- Lifting the Sky
- Archer Draws his Bow
- Plucking the Stars
- Turning the Head
- Wagging the Head and Tail
- Carrying the Moon
- Thrusting Fists
- Lifting the Heels

Closing & Sealing

- Gather your centre
- Pull down the heavens
- Warm the kidneys
- Gently shake
- Breathe naturally

How simple is that?

Final Thoughts

A Student's View

Personal Experience and Thoughts

Anna

My Qigong journey began in 2010. I was being treated by Chris, initially for a marathon training injury and afterwards for other health issues. Chris had mentioned that he was teaching Qigong and suggested I come along to one of his classes to help with my overall health and well-being.

I was intrigued and excited to try this practice which I'd not previously heard of. Chris spoke passionately of it and the health benefits it could bring so I went along. This would be one of the best decisions I'd ever make.

When I look back to that summer, my health was in a bad way. Even though I was physically 'fit' and active from all the (running) training I was doing, emotionally I was trying to deal with some difficult personal circumstances.

I felt like I was falling apart on the inside. I was just holding it together at work in a job I wasn't enjoying which left me feeling exhausted at the end of every day. I was unknowingly neglecting my health, in 'survival' mode, wound up like a spring, not sleeping well and getting through the day on caffeine. I was trying to juggle everything, believing I was looking after my body by all the exercise I was doing, but my physical and mental symptoms were saying otherwise. In hindsight, I was in a constant state of stress.

I will never forget walking away from that first Qigong class I attended with Chris. It was like a weight had been lifted. I felt a sense of calmness that I hadn't felt for a long time. I slept like a baby that night!

It wasn't until the next day that I realised how physical the class had been, even though there was no jumping around and getting out of breath. In fact, my muscles felt akin to having been for a long run the day before, even though for most of the class we had only been stood doing gentle movements.

Any scepticism I had felt about how effective this system could be disappeared after attending my first few classes. I wanted to practise more and learn about this ancient health system I found so relaxing.

Before I share all the considerable improvements that I believe Qigong has made to my health, well-being and happiness, I must say that I haven't always been the ideal student who has practised consistently. I don't mind admitting that I have been my own worst enemy in the past when it came to acknowledging and doing what I know will make me feel better.

Something many students will be able to relate to, I'm sure.

It's an interesting psychology that we can often neglect the very things that will make us healthier and feel better, especially under times of stress and pressure. Qigong is one of the things I should have stuck with, even though in 2012 I moved considerably further away from classes and 'life' got in the way of practising regularly.

A real positive to come out of the periods when I haven't trained regularly over the past six years is that I am now convinced of the ability of Qigong to maintain good health and prevent illness.

I'd like to say it was a deliberate experiment! I don't believe it's a coincidence that my health and zest for life have improved dramatically now that Qigong is firmly in my life. The penny has finally dropped and it's rare that I go a day without training. Even if time is short, ten minutes is still beneficial.

For me personally, I now have a daily practice which can take anywhere between 15 minutes and an hour to complete.

Over the years of training with Chris, I have learned to listen to my body and be aware of how I am feeling physically and emotionally so I can adjust my practice. Some days it really feels like a challenge, some days I can't wait to get out of bed to do my morning Qigong routine.

Commitment, patience and consistency are required. In return for this dedication I can honestly say it is positively life-changing! I've experienced this for myself and have seen it with other Qigong students too.

Where to begin with how my health has improved? My digestion is better and I find my body craves healthier food. I have become much more aware of nutrition and what I put into my body. My energy has increased and my sleep quality is much better and I am much more rested.

I'm sure that Qigong has helped to keep injuries at bay from the high-impact running I do. Before Qigong, I did suffer several running-related injuries in my legs and feet, but since practising regularly, I have almost no aches and pains. This makes all exercise much more enjoyable. It's difficult to put into words, but it feels like everything internally is functioning more efficiently.

Perhaps over and above all the physical improvements, one of the most marked gains for me has been in my mental/emotional health. I'm calmer, less stressed, less reactive and better able to deal with the inevitable challenges that life throws at me. Overall, I'm a much happier person. I feel grounded.

The more time I spend practising, the more the movements flow and feel in harmony with my body. For me, this brings a sense of rhythm within the body, more relaxed breathing and a calming of the mind and nervous system.

I'm now a 'healthy lifestyle' advocate and continue to enjoy the activities I love; running, cycling, yoga and walking my dog. This won't change and Qigong complements all of these. It is so much more than just an 'exercise' system, it's a health system for body and mind. Now that I am studying the theory behind Qigong, I'm beginning to understand how it can prevent disease and maintain optimal health as well as balancing emotions for happiness and contentment.

There's just one catch, you've got to just do it! There's no shortcut for patience and consistency. I've learned that myself. I'm also learning the value of investing those valuable minutes every day and attending classes which I enjoy enormously.

The connection between our bodies and our minds is fascinating! I'm beginning to see why Qigong is so effective. I'm so grateful for the introduction to Qigong and it will always feature in my life. I'm thrilled to be deepening my knowledge and understanding. I hope to share the joy with others and teach one day myself.

My experience of attending classes with Chris is that this system is all-inclusive, anybody can do it, even those with chronic conditions that may prevent them from doing other forms of exercise.

Qigong is not an exclusive club. Students of all ages, shapes and sizes can get practising, it really is for everyone.

The movements aren't difficult to master or highly technical. I cannot recommend Qigong highly enough. It's an investment in health. Don't take my word for it. Try it for yourself.

Marge

About five years ago I was struggling with a very painful shoulder and severe back pain, both of which were having a huge negative impact on my life. I had seen my doctor many times. He gave me lots of different medications for pain, arranged physiotherapy, and finally chiropractic treatment, none of which helped.

Then by chance I met someone who suggested I went to see Chris at his clinic.

They said he helped them and that I should give him a go. What did I have to lose? No one else had helped so how could he, I thought?

I went to see Chris at his clinic. I had Tui Na massage and acupuncture over several sessions. I can honestly say I was able to move my shoulder immediately! For the first time in many years I was able to get up in the mornings pain free which was a big result for me and my life.

During the sessions Chris talked of his Qigong classes and recommended I try them to improve my health.

This was my first step on my Qigong journey, one I will never forget. I can't thank Chris enough for being instrumental in setting me on my way.

I then decided to go along to the Qigong classes that Chris was running every week. I have continued to do this ever since I started six years ago! When I initially started Qigong, I was quite critical of myself as I struggled to get to grips with all the moves. 'What were the Eight Brocades? How was I ever going to master doing them?'

I always used to beat myself up, constantly saying I can't do them. I can remember Chris saying 'practise, practise, and practise'... and how right he was.

I must admit I didn't put the best of effort in to start with. I didn't give it the commitment it deserved, so sure enough that's why I struggled. What I can say is that at some point I had a 'moment' of realisation. I knew I needed to give Qigong my full attention.

The signs were there, so I did it. I stopped beating myself up, I started to practise at least five times a week, listened more to what Chris was saying and started to read more about Chinese medicine. I began to relax and enjoyed the classes more.

There was a period in my life where everything had become increasingly more difficult. I was stressed and felt that challenging and demanding events were taking over my life. This was having an immense impact on my health and well-being. My whole life in general was now becoming affected by this.

I couldn't sleep, was always tired, angry, frustrated, eating healthily was non-existent. I was living on chocolate bars, sporadic meals throughout the day and never had breakfast. I just didn't want to do anything really.

As a result, I took the decision to make a major change to my life which in itself was a bit scary. I know that practising Qigong helped me through this, it kept me calm and safe, gave me inner peace and the internal energy to deal with life-demanding situations. Someone once said to me 'Marge, you are so calm, how do you do it?' and I replied, 'that's the magic of Qigong'.

It has changed my life by enabling me to have a better understanding of my life, my body and what was happening to me as a person. It gave me the confidence and the ability to manage myself and take that step forward into the next phase of my new life.

In February 2016 I was diagnosed with a lifelong disability, a long-lasting auto-immune disease. Although it was good to get a diagnosis after three years of tests, it was also very frightening. The initial fear of the unknown was distressing, a feeling that I could either sink or swim! At this point Qigong became my saviour, it helped me through, completely.

I can honestly say that it has helped me prepare for my future which is going to be different in many ways. Qigong has made me realise the importance of practising and how this helps to maintain my healing and development. Practise helps me to focus on my body as a 'whole'.

So, you might ask, 'what's different?'.

I am pain free, medication free, I have put on weight (I needed to as I was just skin and bone), I now have a warm breakfast every day which has become part of my normal daily routine and I feel so much better for it. I ensure I have meals during the day and some days I am just bursting with energy, to the point where I feel I could conquer the world! I am a lot happier, calmer, I feel good about myself, I believe in myself and my commitment to Qigong.

Listening to what my body is telling me has become easier. I can identify where the tensions are in my body and understand how to change my practice to improve the healing energy around my whole being.

I have a night-time routine that has had amazing results for me. When going to bed I give myself some time to 'check' through my body. This gives me that sense of calmness and relaxation. It has become a true 'mindfulness time' for me and I end up having the best night's sleep ever.

I have noticed that my physical well-being has changed. My muscles are firmer and toned, my skin is softer and better hydrated. My nails are now smooth and shiny, my joints are supple and I find moving around much easier. I can do things now that I could never do before. As a person, I feel really well and healthy, the best I have felt in a long time. It has been so insightful watching me grow, change and develop with Qigong. Awesome.

I am a complete and total believer that Qigong has changed my life and it will always be part of who I am. I send out this message to you all, if you want to change your life, health and well-being, then do what I did and practise Qigong. A decision you will never regret, I promise.

Matt

My Qigong practice over the last four years has made me happier and I walk around with a smile on my face. I feel supported and I have a deeper appreciation of my surroundings, for my life and for my place in the world. Qigong had allowed me to reach that inner place of quiet and peace and this enhances everything else in my life, which means I enjoy life to the full.

I am better-tempered now and less reactive. I was happy before, but I am more fulfilled now. I was stressed and still am sometimes, but I am much better able to manage it. I used to fly off the handle and overreact but now I am much calmer.

In my younger days I was after excitement and stimulation but now I am more content with simple everyday things. I still have back problems but now I am more mindful of them. Qigong alleviates them very quickly.

My practice is also helping me in ways I did not think possible. I want to eat more mindfully and healthily as my tastes have changed. My palate wants cleaner, healthier food and this has also improved my digestion. I indulge occasionally but now I am more aware of what is good for me. This has affected my entire outlook and made me more content with the choice of foods that I am putting into my body.

Physically I have noticed changes too, I feel stronger, with a sense of inner strength. My immune system has improved and so too has my posture. I have looser joints and I am definitely a better dancer!

Qigong has changed my life!

Mandy

Over four years ago, I was having acupuncture with Chris, who told me about his Qigong classes. As a practitioner of Reiki, meditation and all things esoteric, I was intrigued and decided to enrol with my partner. I went with the expectation that I would get fitter, maybe lose a bit of weight and be less stressed.

I am a very busy full-time Head of Drama at a local comprehensive school and this can be challenging at times. Taking up Qigong was one of the best decisions of my life and has changed me in profound ways. I have achieved more balance in my life.

Initially I wanted to read all the books on the subject, but Chris wisely told me to 'practise, practise, practise and it would all unfold'. You 'need to experience it' - I totally understand this now, having gone through the practice in the last four years.

The books I eagerly read now make more sense to me, as I have experienced the many benefits of Qigong for myself on my own path. At the start, my legs shook uncontrollably, I was uncomfortable and I found it challenging at times but with persistence, I am now seeing the amazing results.

Qigong has made me feel more tranquil, energised and healthy, with a deep sense of well-being. I feel less stressed, I am rarely ill, I am more able to cope with the curve balls life can throw at me and I am sleeping better. My mind is calmer and my whole outlook seems more positive and peaceful.

I also feel this is projected onto the people around me. Through my positive presence, relationships are more rewarding. My happy attitude is even more optimistic and joyous.

Feeling fitter from the inside out is a great experience and my body shape is changing for the better. I have a more defined shape and a better posture. As a Drama teacher, I am aware that I speak a lot and I feel that I am starting to listen more and speak less. I am much more mindful about this now.

My energy has increased, my vitality has grown and I now have a great sense of youthfulness. I am suppler and feel strong within my own skin. I am able to face life full on and I am far more effective at work.

People have commented that I look really well and ask me what I am doing. I seem to have a twinkle in my eyes and feel a glow in my skin; far cheaper and healthier than Botox!

My childlike sense of fun and mischief has grown even more. I feel myself wanting to eat more healthily, avoiding chocolate (I was once a chocoholic and ate at least a bar a day!) and alcohol. My digestion is better and as a result I have lost some weight.

This is the first year in my long teaching career that I have not missed a day due to illness so this practice has totally worked for me. My partner and I attend classes together and share our experiences all the time.

This has made us even closer as a couple and I have seen the profound changes in him too. I feel blessed that I found the practice. Qigong is a life changer!

Author's Tip

Qigong brings many different results for each individual and it has become clear to me over the years that the most common effect and the very least of benefits is that Qigong enhances everything!

It just seems to make life better, more enjoyable and joyful again to those that practise regularly. It really is an amazing holistic medicine!

Ready? ... Set? ... GO!

You now have all the information you need to develop a very effective daily practice of Qigong.

You can use it as a daily exercise system to keep you mobile and happy or forge a new pathway on your own personal health journey.

The system shared in this book will keep you happy for many years to come. I myself, as I write this, have used these methods for nearly 14 years and the method still changes and progresses with each practice. As my body and mind grow, the Qigong grows with me, every step of the way. All you have to do is maintain a regular practice and all will be revealed in time.

As previously mentioned, there are many Qigong systems out there if you look, but remember this: gaining new methods, systems or collecting movements will not bring you better health. Being loyal to just one method, will have greater impact and grow with you as you progress through life.

When you practise Qigong, you are actively creating momentum to move forward, to develop the potential to be a better, stronger and more complete human being. It is a system of healing that promotes a natural response within the body and mind to restore and rejuvenate life.

I remember what my life was like before I found Qigong, and all of my illnesses and injuries that led me here to you today!

At two, I fell on my face from an upstairs bannister onto a hard-tiled floor. At six, I fell from a slide and cracked my head open (this was in the early 1980s when slides were really high and without guards).

At eight, my family relocated to a different part of the country which was very stressful. Not long after, I suffered a grand mal epileptic seizure which left me with years of debilitating migraines.

During my teenage years I suffered with anxiety attacks and tendon injuries, experienced periods of depression and the inevitable IBS digestive complaints that seem to come packaged with years of stress.

In my mid-twenties a car accident caused an injury to my neck that never got better despite medications and treatment. After 12 years of suffering with neck pain, sleepless nights and severe relapses, the doctors finally agreed to provide an MRI scan. This led to a visit with a surgeon where I was told that there would be a small chance of losing the use of my right arm if they operated, this was a risk I wasn't prepared to take!

Pain is just pain, an arm is everything! And so I've had to learn to manage the pain myself.

Following a holiday abroad in my thirties, I contracted a virus that lead to three years of chronic fatigue and symptoms of inflammation, which to some extent are still with me now. My symptoms are somewhere between Fibromyalgia and Crohn's disease, the doctors could never really diagnose them properly, so I manage that too.

How do I do it? With Qigong of course!

Since my first experience of Qigong, during my earlier years training in Taijiquan, it has been with me every step of the way. It has led me to train in TCM, acupuncture and Tui Na Massage.

I spent six years training so that I could eventually help others who have suffered like me. In fact, I later opened my own medical clinic so patients could visit for treatment.

Over the years I have visited with doctors who have helped with great advice. I have regular massage treatments and acupuncture. My diet has become balanced, improving my immune system and energy levels. My emotions are vibrant and lively, but calm. Sleep is good, and the future feels exciting.

In amongst all this there has been a constant theme, my Qigong!

It has never let me down and continues to surprise me with the way it maintains and heals me every single day. Life is just so much better now.

If you choose Qigong today, it won't let you down. It can be used alongside any other treatment you are currently receiving. It's like the glue that brings everything together. A real and relevant health practice for modern day living.

So, on that note, I would now like to thank you for reading these pages and hope my words have ignited even the smallest flame within you to now embark on a regular daily practice of Qigong.

Student Notes

Please accept my greatest gratitude

for reading this book

I wish you all the enjoyment and happiness

in your daily practice of Qigong

C. D. Handbury

Further Assistance

If you would like to know more about how to improve your Qigong training, classes and workshops taught by Christopher David Handbury or online training and courses to accompany this book please visit

www.chifitonline.com